Dedication

I dedicate this book to my wonderful wife Patricia; our three wonderful children Brian, Mike and Katie; and our friendly friends—Ben our always very happy dog, who recently became an Angel, and
Buddy, our always cheerful Catholic Cat
who now lives in Cat Heaven.

Thank You All Very Much!

SCOTUS Eliminatus!

No country needs a supreme court that refuses to Hear critical cases! Eliminate SCOTUS ASAP!

Many just recently came to the conclusion that we really do not need a do-nothing Supreme Court. Save budget $$ now & send them home. The Supremes may have been afflicted by a Big Tech Blackout and somehow were the only officials in the country to not know about the big Democrat Election Steal. But the people, with far less resources than SCOTUS know what happened. When the Supremes failed to represent the people the folks in the small places saw a bunch of cowards and wimps saving their own butts from Antifa and BLM and losing the day for America.

Of course they got the news that their vote was important for America. But they would not even hear the case because they already knew how they would have to vote to save their own skins. Where did America find such cowards? So many people have commented on SCOTUS in Chief John Roberts who behaves like the liberal progressive Democrats have threatened him or they have something on him. What is with you Roberts? Either end it or admit you were a failure and change your ways before the people pull the first SCOTUS Eliminatus and fire the whole Court. Save the court by admitting what you did Mr. Roberts. You are not worth much to anybody in the US without a full confession and contrition.

The people know that there are a few potentially OK voices on the court. When Justices did not speak at a time when the people saw the fraud and the steal, they relinquished their claim to be on the Court. Americans were looking to hear from the SCOTUS on this matter for the good of America. Members of Scotus kept the people hanging in despair. They took the job but will not do the hard work, Instead, they give in to their personal fear of a reprisal from either Bully Roberts or Bully Antifa or Bully BLM. Please step down before the time comes when we get to fire your coward butts in a big purge known as SCOTUS Eliminatus. The 80,000,000 plus who voted for the President will not miss you. You all have a target on your backs now for elimination from the Court. Your only hope is to speak up and tell the truth . How can this court above all courts consist of raw cowards.? How can you know of election fraud, be called upon to judge but instead selfishly opt out and damn the country to four years of Chinese Rule. Why should you get another chance SCOTUS. The operative word is ELIMINATUS. Good Bye.

You had a chance with the four states that Texas sued as the tough Texans clearly used a constitutional means attempting to overturn unconstitutional fraud. You can't really think it is OK to steal an election for Biden so fear prevented your acting. Your pusillanimity affected every citizen of the US in every state. Thanks a lot. Big Bully Rogers who ought to eliminate himself rather than the whole court would not permit any of you from discovering the major fraud enough to overturn the elections in all four states. You knew that this would give Trump more than the 270 electoral votes for the win but you failed to act as Justices. All nine of you lily-livered wimps protected yourselves making no decision. You punted leaving America in the lurch. Americans do not need poltroon in the Supreme Court. We are better off with Turkeys than yellowbellies. SCOTUS ELIMINATUS! Amen! Hey SCOTUS You did not give the country a hearing. You should be eliminated without a hearing!

By
B r i a n W. Kelly, M.B.A

Title: SCOTUS Eliminatus!?
Subtitle: No Country Needs a Supreme Court that Refuses to Hear Critical Cases!
Eliminate SCOTUS ASAP!
Author: Brian W. Kelly
Editor,   Brian P.. Kelly
Copyright © 2021 Brian W. Kelly

Referenced Material: *The information in this book has been obtained through many years of study, personal research, practice and observations, interviews, and other methods. Where unique information has been provided or extracted from other sources, those sources are acknowledged within the text of the book itself or at the end of the chapter. Thus, there are no formal footnotes nor is there a bibliography section. Any picture that does not have a source should be considered property of the authors. There may be pictures taken from various sites on the Internet with no credit attached. If resource owners would like credit in the next printing, please email publisher.*

Published by: LETS GO PUBLISH!
Publisher & Editor: Brian W.. Kelly
Mail Location: P.O. Box 621, Wilkes-Barre, PA

Library of Congress Copyright Information Pending
Book Cover Design by Brian W. Kelly; Editing by Brian W. Kelly

ISBN Information: The International Standard Book Number (ISBN) is a unique machine-readable identification number, which marks any book unmistakably. The ISBN is the clear standard in the book industry. 159 countries and territories are officially ISBN members. The Official ISBN For this book is on the outside cover:

978-1-951562-51-9

The price for this work is :   **$14.95 USD**

10   9   8   7   6   5   4   3   2   1

Release Date: January 2021

Acknowledgments:

I appreciate all the help I have received in putting this book together. as well as all of my other 265 other published books.

My printed acknowledgments had become so large that book readers "complained" about going through too many pages to get to page one of the text.

And, so to permit me more flexibility, I put my acknowledgment list online, and it continues to grow. Believe it or not, it once cost about a dollar more to print each book.

Thank you and God bless you all for your help.

Please check out www.letsgopublish.com, our publisher's site to read the latest version of my heartfelt acknowledgments updated for this book. FYI, Wily Ky Eyely, my wonderful young "niece," loves this book and recommends it to all. She wants "Uncle Brian" to be our next US Congressman or US Senator or Wilkes-Barre PA Mayor but Uncle Brian says his days as a candidate are over.

Click the bottom of the Main menu on the site to see the big acknowledgments! Thank you all!

Table of Contents

Preface

Pennsylvania Republican lawmakers and those in all battleground states, whose observers were excluded from observing the vote count, after extensive analysis, found "troubling" discrepancies. Everybody was expecting the supposedly conservative-leaning Supreme Court to make everything right as they often do in such matters of great importance.

"Troubling" unfortunately is a big understatement. At least 74,000,000 plus Americans and my own estimate of 85 million to 90 million Americans ,who had been paying close attention at the time knew that the election had been stolen by overzealous government and privately paid employees who wanted to assure a Biden victory by any and all means possible. Many analysts say that with a fair vote count and without Dominion voting machines, Trump's total would have been far in excess of 80 million. The Supreme Court was well aware of the importance of hearing this case. The do not seem to care about the US any more.

The problems with the election had been widely reported across the country but nobody in the secret counting chambers manned mostly by Democrats seemed to care. It's like they are dress rehearsing for a future job on the Supreme Court. They pulled what can be termed a ballot and vote heist. Every American and that includes the Supreme Court were and are still aware of what was/is going on.

May I repeat that Democrats had one objective—to defeat President Trump and so right or wrong, honest or dishonest, they were pleased with the results. And, so, the Demorats as referred to by those on the other side remained MIA in the foray and they are MIA still today other than to seek impeachment. What can they say since they are not sorry about what they did. On January 20, as we know, it became too late to use the 25th amendment or to conclude impeachment proceedings because, as hard as it is for me to say, Joe Biden was inaugurated as the 46th president. Will it stand? America knows it was a crooked election but for some reason, it may be uncorrectable.

The Austin-American Statesman a Texas newspaper ran a story about how upset Texans are about the SCOTUS' Texas v Battleground SCOTUS decision to no decide. Here is just a little taste of it to whet your appetite on why we don't like the SCOTUS anymore.

"During the electors' debate on whether their resolution should cite the Supreme Court for "moral cowardice," indignant elector Matt Patrick of Dallas took to the chamber's microphone to offer evidence of said moral cowardice. Indignation can be quite effective. There was only one problem with what Patrick said in defense of including the moral cowardice language. And that problem is everything." That says it all"

But the Internet has a lot to say about Roberts: A Supreme Court staffer claims Justice John Roberts 'screamed through the walls' to not take up the Texas lawsuit! He said the justices would have rioters on their front porches. A commenter named Ka Boom offered Roberts counsel: "Roberts should be charged and jailed......period!" I agree

All the while, Americans for Trump had been in earnest believing that the Supreme Court was a real body of judges who cared about America. Americans, even those hoping the Court would not intercede quietly believed that this "fine" Supreme Court would, in the 11th hour, just like when they ruled properly for Bush, would come through for the people. The people of the US had not met the stubborn self-serving scaredy-cat wimp, Chief Justice John Roberts. But they know his name well now as I write this book. His ignominious assault on the American Republic's democratic principles will live on in infamy if not much longer.

In terms of the Supremes acting like the Supremes, folks it was not this time. They were too scared to take the case. My first thought was why did they not become secretaries or carpenters or bus-drivers if they could not take the heat in the kitchen of the highest court in the land. In this book we are going to ask them to get the heck off the Court and choose another occupation for the good of the country. We will use a fine thumping uncle approach to make our point. Hopefully, nobody else will ever have to write a book about nine cowardly justices in anybody's lifetime again.

President Trump was 100% right in his post-facto SCOTUS assessment. The president rarely minces words so he let them have it square-on. President Donald Trump said the Supreme Court "really let us down" by rejecting a lawsuit to overturn Joe Biden's election victory.

Trump tweeted during the unstable period on a Friday night that the justices showed "No Wisdom, No Courage!"

"The Supreme Court really let us down. No Wisdom, No Courage!"
— Donald J. Trump (@realDonaldTrump) December 12, 2020

The President did not have to say it or repeat it as everybody knows the Supremes pulled the product of cowardice from their flowing robes as they feared for their lives because Johnny Roberts, head Justice told them to fear that ANTIFA and BLM would be coming for them if they did the right thing. The reason all nine justices need to be replaced is because not only did they do wimpy Johnny's bidding, unlike Antonin Scalia who would spit on them all if he were alive today.

Nobody even spoke to the press to say they agreed with the president and not the Chief Justice. Cowards! The Cowardly lion had more chutzpah and the Tin man had more heart than these fools who we mistakenly put on the Court of Last Resort. It is time for them to go or begone.

Some people say the Supreme Court's order Friday ended a desperate attempt to get legal issues rejected by state and federal judges before the nation's highest court and subvert the will of voters. The Supremes know they sinned against all Americans.

Democrats want to refer to it as a" *stark repudiation of a legal claim that was widely regarded as dubious, yet embraced by the president,*" Let me say BULL (sh--) Republican state attorneys general and 126 House Republicans are not slouches and they know the law. The Supreme Court may teach the Constitution but they do not live by it when they fear for themselves and not the people.

Trump like most Americans had insisted the court would find the "wisdom" and "courage" to adopt the truth that the election was the product of widespread fraud and should be overturned. The Supremes did not even have the guts to render a verdict on the matter.

The Supremes ignored the fact that the Democrats saw it as a miracle that there were more votes cast than the total number of voters who voted in the 2020. "No problem here." And they saw no issue whenever a spare vote was found, that somehow, it was always a vote for Biden. Great luck! The Supremes do not have the courage to sit on any court anywhere. Please resign so we do not have to create a constitutional crisis as soon as we get the majority or perhaps we can work a deal out with the Democrats before we get the majority.

How about if conservatives trade one Chief Justice Roberts for a Democrat of your choice. How about a Roberts for Merritt Garland trade. Can't be any worse than having Roberts on the court. So, yes, we'd be better off with one less "conservative." At least all the colors will be shown. Oh, you may say that would give Dems a 5-4 majority. For those who think Roberts ever gave Conservatives a 6-3 majority, don't forget about the sale of the Brooklyn Bridge. I heard you can get it for a song. Bye Bye Roberts!

There's a lot more to read folks. We conservatives have been stung and the Supreme Court took sides. What a shame!

About the Author

Brian W. Kelly retired as an Assistant Professor in the Business Information Technology (BIT) program at Marywood University, where he also served as the IBM i and Midrange Systems Technical Advisor to the IT Faculty. Kelly designed, developed, and taught many college and professional courses. He continues as a contributing technical editor to a number of IT industry magazines, including "The Four Hundred" and "Four Hundred Guru," published by IT Jungle.

Kelly is a former IBM Senior Systems Engineer and IBM Mid Atlantic Area Technical Specialist. His specialty was designing applications for customers as well as implementing advanced IBM operating systems and software facilities on their machines. In his position with IBM, he gained substantial writing experience in the preparation of technical documents, run books, proposals, and justification studies.

He has an active information technology consultancy. He is the author of 266 books and numerous technical articles. Kelly has been a frequent speaker at COMMON, IBM expositions, and other technical conferences.

Brian was a candidate for US Congress from Pennsylvania in 2010 and Mayor from his home town in 2015. Brian brings a wealth of experience to his writing and editing endeavors.

Chapter 1 Why Is There a Supreme Court?

Why does the Supreme Court exist?

The proper answer to this question according to legal and government scholars is that the Supreme Court plays a very important role in our constitutional system of government. First, as the highest court in the land, it is the court of last resort for those looking for justice. Second, because it is structured with the power of judicial review, it plays an essential role in ensuring that each branch of government recognizes the limits of its own power. Third, it protects civil rights and liberties by striking down laws that violate the Constitution.

The fourth and final role is that the SCOTUS sets appropriate limits on our democratic government by ensuring that popular majorities cannot pass laws that harm and/or take undue advantage of unpopular minorities. That makes the US a republic and not a pure democracy. In essence, it serves to ensure that the changing views of a majority do not undermine the fundamental values common to all

Americans, i.e., freedom of speech, freedom of religion, and due process of law. Of course when the court determines that taking a critical case is optional, as in the recent election fraud cases, it undermines the people's ability to determine the truth.

That may not sound like a lot of to-dos, but it is an awesome responsibility and one in which courts preceding the current one took quite seriously. The problem with today's court is that they have added the word optional in front of these four main reasons for the court's existence. With all aspects of the court's raison d'etre (reason for its existence) being optional, it means that the court can technically remove itself from any and all of its responsibilities under the Constitution. I am sure that is not what the founders intended.

Because this particular SCOTUS court had fear—a fear of being victimized in a riot because they took the case, the citizens of the US did not find truth or justice. Moreover, it was clearly not the American way for sure. We saw this recently in the cowardly SCOTUS decision not to make a decision in the 2020 Trump Election Fraud.

Origin of SCOTUS

SCOTUS was formed from the most sacred US document—The Constitution. To be specific it came from Article III of the Constitution. This is the Article which establishes the federal judiciary. Article III, Section I states that "The judicial power of the United States, shall be vested in one supreme Court, and in such inferior Courts as the Congress may from time to time ordain and establish."

Although the Constitution establishes the Supreme Court, it permits Congress to decide how to organize it. Congress first exercised this power in the Judiciary Act of 1789. This Act created a Supreme Court with six justices. It also established the lower federal court system. Later it was expanded and contracted and eventually it stuck at nine Justices with lifetime terms as a fair number.

Must SCOTUS take important cases?

Would we all not believe the too-cocky and too-special Supremes would want to take the biggest cases possible to feed their especially large egos. They went through hell to get on the court. Why? So they could punt when a big case came along? No, they wanted the big cases. But they could not believe if they were nominated and selected that there were ugly hearts such as ANTIFA and BLM who would hurt their families and friends and disrupt their neighborhoods if they did their jobs properly.

Consider this. We learned on January 20 how much Congress would pay for its own safety. If the US could pay 26,000 National Guard Troops and 7,000 Biden private troops and countless others in various security roles so the precious inauguration with zero onlookers could go off without violence, could the US not have provided whatever security the SCOTUS needed to do its job without fear? Instead America had to depend on the Supremes being brave enough to do what was right regardless. That is a tall order. SCOTUS was not up to the task.

Nobody can say that the Trump election cases in 2020 were not as big as big ever gets for any country. Leadership is a big thing. But the guy in charge of how the Supremes behave got a case of the yellow belly fever and said he and his family were more important than the country. Yes! He did! Too bad. He did not ask Congress for protection. Why not? He should not have ever taken the job. He hurt the country so badly that he should step down immediately. It should not hurt him since he is not willing to do his job. Chief Justice John Roberts, tell us all why you failed to do what was right for your country? Were you too scared?

Supposedly the Supremes are permitted to take only the important cases and they, themselves get to decide which ones are the most important. Many American people on both sides of the aisle are asking what is more important than the integrity of national elections. Don't we all agree that presidential elections and congressional elections are of the utmost importance to the long term health of our union?

Should we let MSNBC or CNN or NBC and other liberal media outlets make the determination as to which cases are worthy of the Supremes? Should people who may think like me or you be permitted to threaten justices to get our way? Is that what BLM and/or ANTIFA did to scare the hell out of the wimpy coward John Roberts, who few brave men would emulate. If not, would somebody please offer cogent thoughts as to how the people of our country can get our SCOTUS to do its job? Why else do we pay them if not to take the toughest cases?

Why during the election scandal did the Supreme Court appear to be on vacation? When nobody appears ready to stop the steal and tell the truth, should the Supreme Court, which reads the same true press as all of us, intercede with the best wisdom possible. They are the best jurists in the country. If not them, then which impartial body should deliver a ruling on the toughest cases. Before they failed us, who would you have asked to decide the Texas or PA cases other than the supreme minds in the judiciary, who had the Constitutional power to make their rulings stick?

Many of President Donald Trump's allies — both in Congress, in the media and on social media — had called for higher-level intervention into what they alleged was widespread voter and ballot fraud in the 2020 election. Democrats with a lot to gain simply denied that there was any fraud. The truth unfortunately for them did not back them up.

The higher-level we asked for we refer to as SCOTUS but the SCOTUS, because of cowardice and fear, and poor leadership chose not to assist America in its fight. The Supremes knew this was a big fight for truth and justice to fight the biggest election fraud in the history of our country. That should have been a clarion call for the best justices in the land to enlist to determine what was right and what was wrong.

If the media can get an interview with any of the justices of SCOTUS, please ask them if they think that Trump got a fair deal. If you think these weaklings will lie, insist on a lie detector test because the country believes the SCOTUS is corrupt at the top and weak at the bottom.

Unless their families are already at gunpoint, now that it is already too late to save America, why would individual members of SCOTUS not tell the people the truth. Forget about legalese. The Supremes bungled their opportunity and IMHO without a major apology we the people need to call on them to resign and the sooner the better.

Why would they want to pretend they are the best judges in the land when they were too afraid to take the biggest case ever offered to any court anywhere at any time. The truth is this SCOTUS is not worthy of their flowing robes. They disgust me and many other truth loving Americans. .

It got so bad for the people that they sent emails and called into talk shows to ask for U.S. Attorney General Bill Barr to get more involved and according to Breitbart, Fox News host Mark Levin, he and many others had asked that the United States Supreme Court jump into the mix. Levin had warned his viewer constituency over a weekend during the foray that if SCOTUS doesn't get involved, America will face a constitutional crisis. But, Levin at the time believed that the SCOTUS was not overwhelmingly corrupted by self-interests such as self-preservation. Cowards all of them!

Many legal scholars especially of the Never-Trumper ilk attempted to tell the American people SCOTUS had the legitimate right to choose its cases. Then we had the election debacle when SCOTUS failed to act to help promote the truth. They would not even hear all the facts of a case made to order for a Trump victory.

Before then, the regular folks in the country believed 100% in the Supreme Court. No longer. The soft sell of the scholars rang hollow to the people who knew in their hearts that that the SCOTUS had let them down. The SCOTUS abdicated its responsibility to the people and chose through Justice Roberts to remain silent. Why? Cowards!

We the discerning majority overheard that Chief Justice John Roberts was afraid and scared when he was asked to marshal the Supremes to take the right course of action. He feared that rioters and looters would attack him personally and the other justices would not be able to help each other or him in staving off the bad guys.

Of course that would only be if all nine bravely performed their roles as required by the Constitution. They chose not to follow the Constitution as it was too tough a mission to do what was demanded in the circumstances. American wish they would have simply resigned when the job got too tough.

Are Americans supposed to take it on the chin while skittish justices paid by Americans choose not to serve America. Since the people lost big time in the Trump fraud, many now feel they cannot count on a Supreme Court that will opt out of a critical case. It is not an institution that has any value in today's sometimes violent world. If you have no guts, please step down!

How much do Justices get paid?

They get paid a lot—in fact, they get paid more than any other judge in the country. Each judge besides the Chief Justice of the Supreme Court is called an Associate Justice. The annual salary of an Associate Justice for example for 2021 is 268,300. The Chief Justice pockets a handsome $280,500 per year.

At these rates, it is a shame that the biggest cases ever—about a stolen election—were not heard by the highest court in the land. Should we have to pay them an extra bonus to get them to do their jobs or should we fire them because they refused to do their jobs? Technically, the people can decide.

You may know that over the years, various Acts of Congress have changed the number of seats on the Supreme Court, from a low of five to a high of 10. Today it is nine which means unless there is an opening for a Justice, there will not be a tie when they vote.

Shortly after the Civil War, the number of seats on the Court was fixed at the current number of nine. Today, there is one Chief Justice and eight Associate Justices of the United States Supreme Court. Like all federal judges, Justices are appointed by the President and are confirmed by the Senate. They, typically, hold office for life. The salaries of the justices cannot be decreased during their term of office. These restrictions are meant to protect the independence of the judiciary from the political branches of government. None of the founders ever thought they needed a remedy for cowardice.

OK so now we know about them, but they really do not know anything about us. Worse than that, they do not seem to care about us, the hoi polloi of America aka we the people. After all, they emerge in their fine robes and they believe they have achieved the hoity toity enviable position as one of the Supremes.

Who can contravene against a Supreme? Just a person so aggrieved that they will do anything for justice and truth. We all know that. This batch of Supremes are so scared of life and so corrupt because of that, they should resign or be replaced.

The history will show that the SCOTUS kept refusing to take a Trump truth case in the great 2020 Election Scandal to decide definitively. This of course is not America's definition of the function of any court. Meanwhile the state legislatures kept begging to be heard again. Even Mike Pence, who was misguided on his authority, denied the Trump voices in the state legislatures their fair hearing.

The SCOTUS claimed it was a political notion and not for their sparking clean hands to touch. However, none of us, the 75 million unheard, were able to be heard because SCOTUS, our representatives in the case decided to be deaf.. Who can we blame – SCOTUS of course, the wimpiest Supreme Court ever!

Nobody asked a one of US. The SCOTUS was too busy for important national matters because it was scared of ANTIFA and BLM. The people say "Go home and find an ostrich to nest with in the sand. Dear SCOTUS, you deserve nothing better for what you did to America."

Our voices were muted because they, the SCOTUS is made of wimps and they think little to nothing of the people of this country. Tell me why am wrong Mr. or Ms. or Mrs. Supreme SCOTUS? Yes, you disgust Americans and that is why I wrote this book. You disgust many who are happy that I am writing their thoughts.

Who gave the court this power to not follow the needs of the people with its power? Well, the power comes from the Constitution and it was the will of the Founders. It was a good idea when the court could be stocked by good men and women who knew they worked for America. It is no longer a good idea.

To recap, the Court's Jurisdiction comes from Article III, Section II of the Constitution. It establishes the jurisdiction (legal ability to hear a case) of the Supreme Court. The Court has original jurisdiction (a case is tried before the Court) over certain cases, e.g., suits between two or more states and/or cases involving ambassadors and other public ministers.

But most of the time its jurisdiction is not original, it is answering an appeal. Of course the court had its chance when Texas brought forth its law suit. The SCOTUS is the court of original jurisdiction and of last resort when a state sues a state.

On December 8, 2020, in a clever move and a very proper move, Texas AG Paxton sued the Battleground States for what were definite unconstitutional changes to the states' own 2020 Election Laws. Texas Attorney General Ken Paxton filed the lawsuit against Georgia, Michigan, Pennsylvania and Wisconsin in the United States Supreme Court. It was the perfect case of original jurisdiction but the Supremes failed the test because of the scaredy-cat principal. What a bunch of Wimps.

Chapter 2 Can the SCOTUS Read or Understand English?

How big would their scaredy-cat hearts be if we could really see them

Some say, of course and others say if so, they do not understand how these jurists are supposed to be the bravest judges in in the Land? Are they? What would this scaredy cat reflection of the court below have to say about all that? They have already proven that their brave hearts are no bigger than of the furry scaredy-cat below.

If the Justices could all climb into this scaredy-cat, they would fight to be the safest.

The SCOTUS has not answered that deep question about bravery. There is no question about that. They do not have a clue. Does courage live in the heart or the mind? What compels some people to turn toward danger and others to run away when frightened? I would suggest that the nine Supremes consult with science writer Jeff Wise for the answer. Maybe he can tell them how to muster up enough courage to do their jobs.

Wise studies and writes about such factors. For example, he has the answer to why some people act quickly, who are willing to take a risk for a stranger? He knows what makes them tick and why some would run toward danger rather than away from it?

If a five-year old were locked in a car in an icy cold stream minutes away from having no air, after reading this story, I know that Jeff Wise would be sure that without his course, he would expect that none of the nine members of the present SCOTUS would jump into the water to save the boy. The little boy would then die of suffocation while the SCOTUS breathed on. Sorry Charlie SCOTUS, you had your chance and failed. Thank God a little boy did not die. A woman jumped in and saved him. He did not die --just a country – our country, the USA. How does that make you feel SCOTUS?.

The only excuse for cowardly supreme court justices is that they did not know what was going on. They may not have read the papers or listened to or saw the news. But, if they really did not know what was going on in their world, with their important jobs, would they not be judged to be stupid? Are they stupid or do they simply protect their own hide instead of choosing to do what is best for Americans—the people who pay their salaries..

For my money, and a lot more, they should ease their pain permanently and resign. No excuse is a good enough excuse for their cowardice. We Americans do not want to live with their dumbness or ignorance or coyness or selfishness. Beat it SCOTUS. Get lost. My kind sister might suggest a long walk on a short pier but rather than become martyrs for cowardice, SCOTUS should simply remove themselves from their responsibilities.

Dear Supremes, your voluntary departure would be fine for lots of Americans who last saw you in action or should I say inaction. Pitiful! Are you at least embarrassed? Of course Democrats may think differently as they enjoy their unearned spoils. What a shame how this court appears to all the great jurists who came before them. They are too blind or too scared to serve America and honest Americans . They can make up for it by going home permanently. Good by!

The Trump campaign and affiliates and unaligned legal helpers of America, subsequent to the election day debacle accepted and/or enlisted the help of litigation boutiques from around America to help the President reclaim his stolen win. The Supremes knew he was the victim of a major theft and that they were the only body that could make it right. It did not matter to them.

Nobody expected that the Supreme Court would choose not to do its job. Those pressing them were individual attorneys. as well as a handful of small law firms. Most were already conservative favorites. Their mission was to find the fraud and file lawsuits in several ground zero battleground states . These were the states in which vote counts despite reality, somehow always favored Joe Biden.

In some litigation, the Trump campaign also leaned on litigation support from Am Law 200 firm Porter Wright Morris & Arthur. But large law firms, in general, had not played a prominent role in representing Trump in post-Election Day litigation. They like the SCOTUS were a bit weak in the knee.

Those watching NewsMax, OAN, and listening to the finest in Talk Radio from Rush Limbaugh etc., suggested from the beginning that some of the most consequential litigation was to be focused on Pennsylvania. For example, campaign lawyers filed a U.S. Supreme Court motion to intervene in a dispute regarding the counting of absentee ballots received after Election Day.

Notables such as Newt Gingrich weighed in suggesting that unobserved ballots should simply not be counted. The deeply afraid Supreme Court offered little and Americans concluded they were deaf, dumb, blind, and incapable of holding a productive job (employment).

Listed as the counsel of record in the PA Supreme Court motion were Jay Alan Sekulow, of the Constitutional Litigation and Advocacy Group, and Consovoy McCarthy attorneys Patrick Strawbridge, William Consovoy and Thomas McCarthy. All are sharp as a tack lawyers and if they could ever find a fair court to hear their arguments, they would be likely to win the day based on the facts. The truth does not lie. Perhaps the scared Supremes had a right to fear the Trump team.

In the first dispute before the Supreme Court, Jones Day partner John Gore, former Trump-era principal deputy assistant attorney general in the U.S. Justice Department's civil rights division, represented the Republican Party of Pennsylvania, in its attempt to undo a Pennsylvania Supreme Court ruling about whether the extension of the deadline for mail-in ballots was legal. It was not legal but the ineffective and afraid SCOTUS would not permit themselves to hear about it.

There is a difference between being legal and being constitutional. This deadline did not meet the constitutional smell test and thus was illegally declared legal.

Many of us remember Jay Sekulow as being well known for representing Trump in his first impeachment battle. Great lawyer, but, he had a real court which heard his arguments then. Our too busy SCOTUS refused Sekulow even though he had the evidence cold.

These forays against dishonest Democrats are not being fought pro-bono and that's why there were so many concurrent fund-raisers. For a while I know half of the emails in my in-box were requests to help finance this effort. The Supremes did not care what America spent to get them to hear the case. But, I cared enough to donate as much as I could. How about you?

The defenders of liberty and freedom needed funding. Maybe the Supremes did not think they were being paid enough to take the people's cases in the fight against nationwide election fraud. We all know that Lawyers, even bad lawyers do not come cheap. Sekulow's firm for one has received $660,000 from the Republican National Committee since October 2019, according to FEC records, and Consovoy McCarthy—the firm on the front lines of Republicans' pre-election litigation—has billed Trump's campaign and the RNC for nearly $2.5 million since last October when they began to prepare for the inevitable.

The Supremes IMHO received their normal rate, which is almost $300K per Justice per year for doing their normal job but they did not do their normal job. They chose not to help America. I think America should ask for a refund from these folks who are too rich to care.

Consovoy reportedly has a rate of $950 per hour so any funds that come in to help Trump were more than likely spent on the legal part of the stolen election effort. Heck, when America is at stake, even the poor will contribute to help America win. Perhaps the Supremes were looking for more than what is right and just to urge them to take a case that affected America.

Perhaps somebody got to them , threatening them one way or another. Hey, they took the job. In fact, the literally fought all their lives for this particular job. Should we not have expected them to do the job once they got it.

The people are not ready to give these cowardly Supremes another chance no matter what their reason for squinching America. They think they are so great, that none of them addressed the people to tell us why they did what they did even though they knew that it hurt the country. They are not great at all. Cowards are nothings—we all know that.

While there are official lawyers contracted by the Trump team, many conservatives see Rudy Giuliani, the president's personal attorney as one of, if not *the* key player in a public role in the SAVE AMERICA scenario. Other great lawyers who care about the truth include Sidney Powell and Lin Wood, a great attorney who first attracted media attention when he took on the Richard Jewell case.

The Supreme Court gets paid whether it helps America or not. This group of Jurists, and I use the term loosely ,punted and we should punt all nine of them off the court in a sonic boom. Hand me the ball first, please. I would be pleased to boot it and them all out of the park.

People with a stake in the Trump win steal came forward. They put their lives at stake and on hold, and under threat of prosecution, they swore to their statements under oath. The Supremes did not care or they would have as a group or individually with robes on or off, offered their commentary to tell the people why they behaved in such a cowardly fashion.

You may recall that Richard Jewell was a security guard who was falsely accused in what became known as the Centennial Olympic Park bombing in Atlanta back in 1996. Wood's work on the case helped him become one of the most prestigious lawyers in the country. The Supremes would not give Powell or Wood or anybody who cared a hoot for the country even a hearing. They are despicable as I see it. They gotta go.

Overnight after his success with the Jewell case, Lin Wood went from being a run of the mill personal injury lawyer to a nationally known defamation lawyer. And, Lin Wood is not only good, as an attorney, just like Tony the Tiger, he's Great!

Does the SCOTUS think it is served by the people or does it think it serves the people? These pompous dimwits see nothing but their own skins. My case v SCOTUS is closed but I continue because we have to rid ourselves of their scourge.

Sidney Powell & General Michael Flynn.

Most conservatives are familiar with the dirty deal given to General Michael Flynn. He was President Trump's first choice for National Security Advisor. Hillary Clinton paid for Flynn to be crushed by the FBI. Sidney Powell worked successfully to discover the Clinton connection after hope was lost to have the Justice Dept's charges dropped against Flinn.

The Supremes observed all of this and still let it stand. My kids had a word for this when they were kids, which fits more than it sounds like it fits—POO-TINK! That's about as good a phrase as can be conjured up to describe the conduct of the SCOTUS and Hillary Clinton in this case.

Sidney Powell is a well-known Dallas defense lawyer who "rode into Washington" determined to exonerate retired Army Lt. Gen. Michael Flynn. Her forte is to unearth stashed evidence and prosecutorial misconduct in resolving cases for the benefit of her clients.

She originally came to fame in the Enron scandal and afterwards. she wrote a book about how corrupt she believes the U.S. Justice Department actually is. I have not heard anybody speak well of the SCOTUS in their recent "efforts" in the biggest corruption ever in US elections. Have you? They are a definite disgrace.

Sidney is respected by a lot of people who do not pay her salary as the SCOTUS, all public-paid, including the newest, Amy Cony Barret (ACB), overrated, who as of today have labeled Mouse Peep. She said nothing and did not even make a mouse peep in support of a person who made her a candidate. Mouse Peep is the highest accolade I can give any member of the court as it exists today. It is a waste.

Powell is very well received by conservatives many of whom are like me and think like she does. Well Sidney came back in town again whether the Trump campaign wanted her or not. She helped. officially or unofficially. She cared and helped President Trump and the team, like it or not, in resolving matters about the stolen election for the president. If the SCOTUS did its job, Donald J. Trump would be in his fifth year as president. Maybe John Roberts simply did not like him.

Sidney Powell did more for America than the American Supreme Court who did what my friends as kids would say *did squat*. Nobody who I know contests that assertion. The Supremes are highly overrated and the ND Dame is the highest overrated justice on the court. Nobody. Other than John Roberts said she had to be quiet about what she thought about the elections. So if it were not an order, it was her own decision to not help America. Thanks a lot Ms. Mouse Peep!

I am impressed with Sidney Powell much more than ACB because Powell has to work for a living. So does General Michael Flinn. I suspect Barrett would not help him if it were any work on her part even if she could. Why try to get a job that you refuse to do to the best of your ability? Barrett, you are my biggest disappointment. Still not a word. Poo Tink Mouse Peep!

A good part of the facts in this book come from work done by the aforementioned Sidney Powell, a renegade lawyer who wants American justice like many of us, unlike a deaf, dumb, and a blind SCOTUS.

Most people have functional brains. Those with such brains know that Trump had an election stolen from him in broad daylight. Regardless of the team of lawyers the president had officially working the case, many of us were very happy that Sidney Powell was also on the job. SCOTUS seemed to have been hired by George Soros and the Democrats or perhaps the Demorats, a more fitting term. What am I missing?

Maybe Amy will send us some enlightenment such as the reason for her own personal cowardice and non-committal attitude. I bet others who supported her candidacy now think like my kids did when they had one way to describe bad stuff – POO TINK! Yeah Amy Barret is POO TINK. Amy, if you think I am wrong see what other conservative kids think. Is it POO TINK? I bet it is.
Step down please! As soon as possible!

Chapter 3 Bush v Gore & A Cowardly 2020 SCOTUS

CNN

CNN SPECIAL REPORT

BUSH v. GORE:
THE ENDLESS ELECTION
MONDAY, NOVEMBER 2 9$^P_{ET/PT}$

On December 9, 2000 the U.S. Supreme Court aka SCOTUS, showing the world that it was separated by either ideology or truth, put a stop to the vote counting in Florida and thus set the stage for a ruling that would ultimately make George W. Bush the next president. In retrospect maybe he did not deserve it. He was not such a good president. But as a conservative, I found him a lot better than Al Gore would have been,

Was it close? You bet it was. The SCOTUS decision was by a vote of 5-4. Just one day prior, in fact just 22 hours prior. the Florida Supreme Court made its final ruling. Looking back over twenty-years, the Florida Court before the SCOTUS intervened, had required new hand counts of the presidential ballots. It was clear that this approach favored Gore. However, when Scotus overruled the Florida court, their action immediately jeopardized Vice President Al Gore's chances of overtaking Bush. Thankfully that did not matter to the court.

They took it even further by agreeing to hear the Bush challenge to the state decision. It set a hearing, to run 90 minutes, for 11 a.m.

December 11, 2000. To the pundits and onlookers alike, this ruling was a sign that the Florida court's count ruling was in jeopardy.

One SC Justice in the majority, Antonin Scalia, whose sage counsel was missing in 2020 suggested that the action meant a majority believed that Bush "had a substantial probability of success" in his challenge. It was expected the same five justices would see things Bush's way when they made their final ruling.

At the time of course, there was no ANTIFA or BLM or other potential rioters to disturb the home life or threaten the SCOTUS justices in the year 2000. In retrospect, some may see the potential for home protesting of the justices by radical groups who hate Trump as what caused the 2020 court favor to tip towards the other side. The court ultimately decided not to hear the Trump case which was their cowardly way of saving their own bacon.

The four "Democratic liberal progressive leftist" dissenters in the case of George W. Bush vs. Albert Gore Jr. also said that the court's action to halt the counting was tantamount to a decision" in favor of Bush.

Enter James A. Baker III. He took the place of Rudolph Giuliani as Bush's chief legal strategist in Florida. Obviously the Texas governor was "very pleased" by the court's action but he was concerned that the dizzying month of ups and downs was not over because the court had not yet ruled on the merits of the case.

You may recall Gore's lead attorney, David Boies, who we saw on TV frequently during this period. He publicly remained optimistic that the vice president (Gore) would ultimately prevail but he saw that the Supreme Court's taking the case and acting on it, made it "much more difficult" to complete the vote count by Dec. 12. In Florida, that was the date by which Florida was to have finished picking its 25 presidential electors. That Florida number was enough to give either candidate the White House.

Bush's lawyers had asked the court to stop the counting, saying it threatened to "imperil" his "proper receipt" of Florida's electoral votes and could wipe out his certified victory. Gore's attorneys did not buy their argument and insisted that Bush had suffered no legal harm from the counting and that if he did suffer anything, he could return to court with his next constitutional challenge.

It was a close race and every chad counted. Bush's Florida margin stood at 154 after the Florida Supreme Court ruling a few days earlier on Friday afternoon. The Bush campaign and the Gore campaign remained at odds about who had made gains during the recount this day before the Supreme Court shut the count down. Things did not look good for Gore after the count had been shut down

The Supreme Court was very agreeable in hearing the Bush appeal even before they had technically filed their case. In fact, the court appeared ready to give Bush the victory immediately after the Texas governor's "emergency application" for a temporary stop to the counting. The SCOTUS treated it like the appeal itself, and basically granted it. SCOTUS liked Bush but did not like Trump. Too Bad for the people.

There was no John Roberts, a backstabbing wimpish conservative who was a Democrat in Sheep's clothing. Roberts, in my humble opinion has some sort of personal vendetta against Trump to direct the court his way. The Bush/Gore case was taken up as it should have been without John Roberts mucking it all up.

The court took up the case and ruled based on its merits. The seemingly corrupt Roberts was not there to be overheard screaming at the lesser justices to adjust their thinking on the merits.   What a difference twenty-years makes. In 2000, the Supreme Court was a viable required institution. The conscientiously without politics took up the cases that were appropriate. Now, the court is so afraid of its collective shadow that all members should resign. That remove the court from its own corruption and misery.

Gore was not in the Driver's seat in this appeal but there was no cheating alleged in Florida either. A positive Gore outcome appeared to be a long shot. Even the VP's attorneys privately said that their cause would be in considerable trouble if the court ordered a stop— even a temporary halt—to the counting. Which, of course is what happened. They conceded it would be a sign of the court's tilting toward Bush's ultimate claim that he would be harmed if the counting went on.

The account was written like this "Today's order by the U.S. Supreme Court contained no explanation as to why a majority was blocking continued counting or why it was willing to hear Bush's challenge." The SCOTUS seldom explains such actions. However, the great and honorable Justice Scalia broke with custom and offered his point of view without saying whether the other four in the majority agreed with him. Scalia did note that it "is not customary for the court to issue an opinion in connection with its grant of a stay" - that is, an order to stop an action.

In the majority that approved the order, along with Scalia, were Chief Justice William H. Rehnquist and Justices Anthony M. Kennedy, Sandra Day O'Connor and Clarence Thomas, the court's four other most conservative members. Remember those names.

Justice John Paul Stevens, the court's senior associate justice, spoke for the four dissenters, the court's bloc of liberals and moderates that also includes Justices Stephen G. Breyer, Ruth Bader Ginsburg and David H. Souter.

The Start Date as they call it for the courts final ruling was on December 12. 2000. The Supreme Court, in what was known as a per curiam opinion, ruled that the Florida Supreme Court's decision, calling for a statewide recount, violated the Equal Protection Clause of the Fourteenth Amendment. This ruling was by a 7–2 vote, though per curiam opinions are usually issued only for unanimous votes. In other words, per curium normally means unanimous. It is typically by decision of a judge, or of a court in unanimous agreement.

This case was often referred to as the "hanging chads" as it was the first time punch card ballots had been used in Florida. Law scholars differ on the similarities of Bush V Gore and the Trump cases . They suggest that the standards for counting the infamous "hanging chads" which were incomplete marks on those punch card ballots, varied from county to county. This is almost by definition unequal protection under the law.

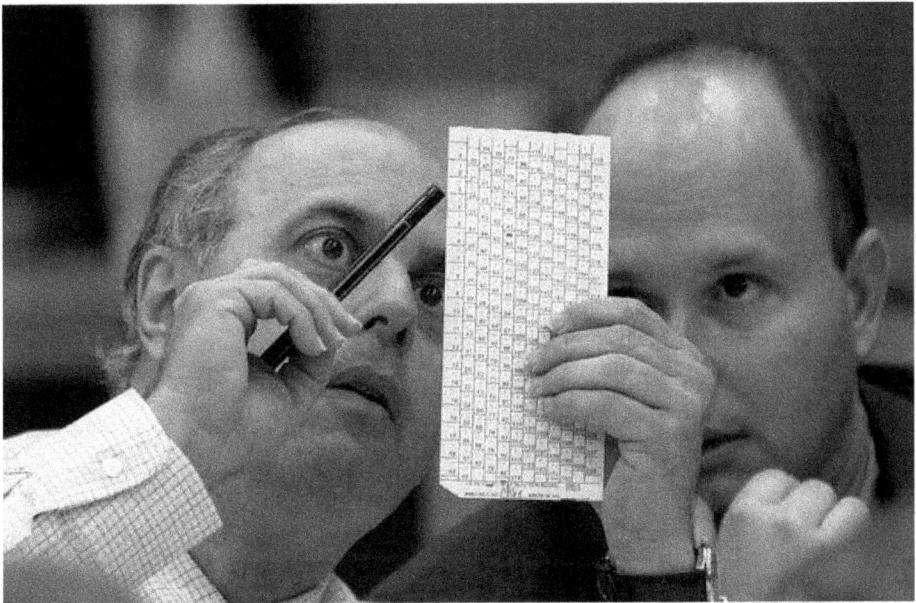

The U.S. Supreme Court held that this lack of uniformity violated the Equal Protection Clause of the Constitution, which guarantees equal weight for all votes. As we just recounted, the court ultimately properly shut down the recount and declared Bush, the Republican candidate, the winner in Florida – and therefore of the 2000 election.

Republicans used what they saw as a precedent to try a similar play in Pennsylvania with a legal claim they filed on Election Day. Pennsylvania was not as organized as Florida. For example, in some Pennsylvania counties, election officials were contacting voters whose mail-in ballots had already been disqualified for technical reasons. They tried to confirm their signature or fill in missing identifying information, to validate their ballot so it could and would count. They called this "ballot curing." However, not all PA counties were curing ballots. Trump's lawyers argued that the state's lack of uniformity violated the Equal Protection Clause. They were right but a court that does not follow its own precedents is a worthless court indeed.

Trump had another Pennsylvania legal challenge, from September 2020 . It too was rooted in Bush v. Gore. It relied on an often overlooked concurring opinion in that case. This opinion was an alternate theory for explaining the Bush win. It was written by Chief Justice William Rehnquist as a supplement to the majority decision. Its basis was because of what is called the "plenary authority" of state legislatures to allocate Electoral College votes. It claimed that PA had violated the US Constitution.

You see under Article II of the Constitution, state legislatures and only state legislators can make important electoral decisions. In other words, the state legislators have total power to decide to whom and how their Electoral College votes should be awarded. The Constitution says they don't even have to hold a presidential election if the state legislators do not want to.

Whatever their process, Rehnquist wrote, the Constitution demands that it be respected. No court, state or federal, should disturb their decision.

Ironically, though the notion of "plenary authority" is not controversial and it should have been Trump's path to victory with a properly functioning SCOTUS, Rehnquist's concurrence may very well be viewed as a pro-Gore legal opinion.

In it, the Chief Justice argued that by ordering an emergency recount whose timing and deadlines deviated from the legislatively provided election rules, Florida's Supreme Court was usurping the Florida legislature's plenary authority. Interesting! But his opinion did give the current SCOTUS a rationale for deciding in Trump's favor. But, the court did not follow the truth and opted to follow Roberts' wishes by punting on the issue.

Admittedly some lawyers think that the "Article II theory" is on the rather fringe – but the cowardly SCOTUS did not even examine it in Pennsylvania. They will have plenty of time to read the opinions of real SCOTUS justices when through the miracle of SCOTUS Eliminatus, they are permanently retired.

Chapter 4 Can the Supreme Court Ever Be Trusted Again?

Would it not be good if a real person such as Juice Scalia could come back from the dead and guide the wimps of SCOTUS:

The new Supremes do not understand that this is important

If you strike out in the bottom of the ninth with the bases loaded while losing by two runs, would your fans be justified in asking you to find a new job. I hope all the Supremes who chose not to help America can find jobs or can retire. They made a big mistake no matter what their reason. I do not care what their backgrounds are; their hearts are woo weak and their courage is too lacking for America to ever trust them again. Sayonara to the nueve. They have given up being justices based on their behavior in their biggest opportunity ever. sayonara to each and every one of the nueve.

She is very good.

Sidney Powell is clearly one of the top lawyers in America but there are some lawyers on the Trump team who would prefer to not have her watchful eye on them. There are a number of conservatives who think with advice like theirs, Joe Biden could get four years of unimpeded bliss. My advice to them was to do their own jobs and let Sidney Powell go on unimpeded to bring in a win for the president. Sometimes a rigged process cannot be undone regardless of whether it is discovered or not. Keep reading. An honest court is a prerequisite, not six conservatives voting as liberals.

It's tough to have a White House full of Never Trumpers, yet the president was stuck with a crew that he could not trust. So, he was often forced to do things for his own good rather than to please his staff.

Such was the rationale for a meeting at the White House a few Friday's ago in which President Trump seriously weighed appointing Sidney Powell, as his "man" on the scene to investigate voter fraud. It would have been a short-term position as Trump's reelection did not occur. Nonetheless, his "loyal" WH team was not so happy about that and they leaked disinformation about the meeting like as if Powell promotes conspiracy theories about rigged voting machines. Dah! And who thinks they were not rigged?

Unsolicited advice to the president—Next time in office, get rid of the staffers that are not on your side.

With the backlash from staff, it was still unclear as I wrote this the first time and had to update it after January 6. Mr. Trump did not l move ahead with such a plan. My advice of course would have been to take Powell, who has proven her worth far more than White House Never-Trumper staffers and make good use of her talents.

Rudy Giuliani it is said, joined the meeting discussion by phone initially, while Ms. Powell was at the White House for the meeting. As might be expected when somebody finds somebody more qualified being hired, the meeting became raucous and involved people shouting at each other at times, according to one of the people briefed on what took place.

Ms. Powell's client, retired Lt. Gen. Michael T. Flynn, the former national security adviser whom the president recently pardoned was also there at the same meeting showing his support for Ms. Powell for the post. This is according to two of the people briefed on the meeting. Some senior administration officials drifted in and out of the meeting. Their senior official days ended soon after along with the end of Trump's term.

Sidney Powell is about as good as the President can get to help his cause. When she engages, she wins. She does not quit. I regret along with many conservatives that somehow we let a crooked election determine who our president is going to be for the next four years. What a shame. Thanks a lot SCOTUS.

She kept at it a little longer in her independent quest to bolster the claims of election fraud with facts and affidavits. She knows and many conservatives have seen the proof that there was an algorithm developed by Democrats to switch votes in the Dominion machines from Trump to now President-elect Biden, soon President Biden. None of that seems to matter now as it appears over. I thought I heard a lady with my waist size singing on January 19.

I know that my favorite conservative attorney Sidney Powell withdrew her lawsuit in the U.S. Supreme Court challenging Georgia's election results Tuesday, January 19. It was her second to be voluntarily dismissed, as the legal campaign to overturn President

Donald Trump's election loss has petered out in the waning days of his term. Tomorrow (Jan 20 it is all over I guess) Thanks a lot SCOTUS.

Unfortunately for the Democrats, their plot was discovered because their algorithm broke down because of unprecedented strong support for Trump on election day. The cheaters did not know they would need to manufacture from thin air, so many extra votes due to the fact that Trump had skunked Biden in the real true election. But, there was no way to adjudicate the truth. And it is all over now— even attempts to prosecute the perpetrators except in Arizona.

For a while, it looked good but SCOTUS ultimately shut it all down. In order to make up for this error, Sidney Powell has the proof and has presented much of the proof along with Atty Lin Wood. The conclusion reasonable people have made is that the Democrats manipulated the vote with mail-in ballots. In the battleground states of our nation, Democrat election workers across the country were knowingly or unknowingly involved in this fraud scheme. What happened in this election could not have happened happen by accident. Even SCOTUS new and that is why CJ Roberts was overheard screaming at his fellow justices.

During the Trump stolen-election period from election day through January 20, a lot of one-time Trump allies switched sides also. They switched to Biden. This included Fox News and some hosts in particular such as Tucker Carlson who must have gotten word from the new FOX owners to stop being so favorable to Trump. So, he did.

Carlson is now on my S-list. My brother says he seems to have changed his tune in late January. He was one of the first to pick a fight with Sidney Powell claiming she had no evidence. After I checked out the show again, I joined conservatives who figured Tucker and Fox were no longer important to us.

There is **no evidence** that we have seen to prove us wrong. And there is a lot of evidence to back up the switch in allegiance from Fox News to other networks and news outlets. My two choices are now NewsMax and AON. The other networks do not have the two liberal Murdoch sons guiding their slippery hands.

Some call it a new class of conservative outlets and networks that have raced each other to capture the attention of disgruntled Trump voters. That describes my own reaction to my observations of post-election Fox. They no longer needed Trump. I no longer need them.

Most conservatives right after the election felt abandoned by traditional conservative news companies such as Fox and Tucker Carlson and it was not a good deal being censored by social media.

Fox News once owned conservatives because of their conservative programming but after the Murdock boys took over for dad, unexpected changes such as Donna Brazile appearing on the network shows. Conservatives noticed right away but hoped it was an aberration and not a new policy.

It is true that there's a race unfolding among several conservative outlets who don't think Fox is pro-Trump enough. It isn't and Fox is paying dearly with diminished viewership. Fox is not the only game in town any more. My Fox viewership is down about 85%. Rather than watch turncoat Chris Wallace's pretend sincerity. Sorry Chris. Good-bye Chris.

After the election, former conservative favorites like Breitbart, Drudge Report and Real Clear Politics and yes, Fox News, began to lose traffic share to Newsmax, OAN, and Gateway Pundit, according to data from web analytics company. These new entries are beginning to eat full lunches at the former favorites' expense.

Some real statistics include the fact that in recent weeks, Newsmax overtook Breitbart to become the most visited right-leaning news site. TV ratings for Newsmax TV have surged. NewsMax and OAN are not going away. Their— marquee host Greg Kelly recently has been drawing as many as 1 million viewers a night. All of this is happening while President Trump continues to urge followers to abandon Fox News. Most of us are listening. If Trump does not like Fox anymore, why should any of us?

In the next several weeks we hope to see what the new Trump mission is all about. I sure hope he works with a good legal team to straighten out the US election system. There is no sense voting again if the election thieves are not punished.

Rush Limbaugh substitute hose Todd Herman asked Powell during a recent interview, "Imagine you find yourself in an elevator with five Supreme Court Justices, and it's a long elevator ride. Say, you've got 90 seconds to convince them to actually hear your evidence. How would you proceed Atty Powell? Powell has the evidence. To remind you of her altercation with Tucker Carlson, even after Powell's extensive expose, Carlson pulled the left's most asked question: "Where is the evidence." Tucker, you definitely don't want my answer to your Smart-Alek lefty question. .

Attorney Sidney Powell responded and the transcript from the show follows? She explained it in no uncertain terms. You want evidence -- follows in 9 seconds, here you go!

Sidney Powell in 90 seconds"

Before your eliminate the SCOTUS, how about reading Sidney Powell for the next ninety seconds. Then, you will know how wrong you are on what you should have done. .

"The very night of the election many people saw something they had never seen before in the history of our elections. They saw votes being changed on the screen in front of them, going from President Trump to Mr. Biden. No kidding!

On top of that, the morning after the election, even that night, the voting stopped. [unprecedented in multiple states], They stopped counting in multiple districts at the same time before the vote got to 270 electors for President Trump. That's never happened before in history.

The only time votes have ever stopped being counted in this country on election night was when the Broward County problem developed over the Hanging Chad's in one county in FL. So for five states to stop counting on election night is absolutely unprecedented.

[Why would they stop counting?]

And they did it because the vote count for the electoral college was about to hit [+ go over] 270 for President Donald Trump, because of the massive outpouring of votes for him that night. By the next morning, multiple mathematicians had contacted me (Sidney Powell) and told me they knew the algorithm that had been run to change the votes.

It was that obvious to people with mathematical expertise. It is a mathematical impossibility for 100's of thousands of votes to show up in the middle of the night for Vice President Biden alone, and to have been injected into the system the way that they were."

We have eye-witness testimony of countless people who saw votes coming in, in unsecured containers and improper means, and looking different the night of the election. These people have come forward at great personal risk to themselves and their families to provide thousands of affidavits of voting abnormalities and actual crimes that they witnessed happen on election night. The very fact that the other side is working so hard to hide all of this. Federal law requires transparency in our electoral process and our elections.

There is a federal statute that requires all the documents pertaining to elections to be maintained for 22 months following an election, for the very reason that it has to be completely auditable. A Federal Judge in October in Atlanta, found all kinds of problems with the Dominion system that GA bought and crammed down for everybody across the state to use. That's where the most problems have been, is in Georgia.

Witnesses have come forward, there was supposedly a water leak that they shut down voting for. That was an abject lie. We have video of witnesses pulling suspect ballots out from under a table after they ran off all the observers. Somebody told me that one of the people that did that has told government officials, how it happened and what happened.

But has that information been provided to the public? No. There is rampant voter fraud of all kinds. Federal violations of 5 years and more across the country by virtue of all the misconduct on election night.

The flipping of votes by Dominion is even advertised in their ability to do that, to run a fraction, to make a Biden vote count 1.26% and a Trump vote to only count 0.74%. They've done it before. They've done it in Venezuela. They done it in other foreign countries. They've done it in this country. We have evidence even that it was done in 2016 in California to benefit Hillary over Bernie [Sanders], and it's been done in other local elections and smaller elections different places.

This is the only time it's been this widespread, and the reason it didn't work this time, they've been able to shave these votes for a long time, but the reason it didn't work completely this time and they had to shut down in so many places was because so many Trump supporters poured out on the day of the election to vote for President Trump in what was a landslide victory, a historic victory, is because it broke their algorithm.

That's why they had to stop counting that night. That's why they had to bring in ballots and try to back-fill. And it still doesn't work, because there's still 100's of thousands more votes than there were voters to vote them. The math simply doesn't add up. And if they had nothing to hide, why aren't they providing transparency into the voting systems of the United States of America, the country that is founded upon the Rule of Law and is supposed to be above all this?

It is absolutely the most appalling criminal operation in the history of our country.

End of Sidney Powell's Ninety Minutes on Election Fraud prompted by Todd Herman

We have a lot more in this book starting in the next chapter about Sidney Powell's evidence.

As a North Carolina Native, growing up in the Triangle, Sidney Powell says that she never missed an episode of Perry Mason. Nor do I. I watch it every day and I learn something on each repeat show.

Now she's starring in what many say is her own prime-time legal drama. But it has been way more than that.

On a Thursday in November after the election, Sidney Powell stood alongside former New York Mayor Rudy Giuliani. Together, they argued for 90 minutes that President Donald Trump had won the election in a landslide,. only to have the results marred by fraud.

Anybody who has used their brain in 2020 knows that when it smells like a dead fish, it is probably a dead fish. This whole stinky fraudulent election is the fishiest smelling election of all time.

" We are going to reclaim the United States of America for the people who vote for freedom," said Atty Sidney Powell, part of what Giuliani calls Trump's elite strike force team.

It ain't over 'til it is over and Trump is the acclaimed winner.

Even if he is not so declared, we all know he won by a landslide.

Defeat the Media and the Democrats is our new theme song!

While we are all regrouping we know in our hearts with the machine mis-tabulations, our guy Trump had between eighty million and Ninety Million votes – unprecedented.

Being unpunished for the theft of the election, conservatives know the Bidon show is a fake show and he did not earn the presidency. A corrupt SCOTUS awarded it to him by not doing their jobs.

Chapter 5 Watch to Whom You Hitch Your Wagon.

Tucker Carlson is still feeling the heat from former Fox allegiants. He's getting barbs typically reserved for Humpty Dumpty at CNN— **Traitor, Globalist, & Sellout.** Why? Simple!

Because he sold out conservatives seemingly for a better payoff with the Murdoch twins. What else could it be? No apologies and he was belligerent to Sidney Powell. If you had your horse and wagon hitched up to Fox and Tucker Carlson. Feel free to find a new hitching post.

Carlson threw Sidney Powell Under the Fox Bus!

Traitor. Globalist, & Sellout, etc. were not the worst of what Tucker Carlson was called when he put himself before his viewers by slamming Sidney Powell for no apparent reason. He diminished her work on bringing Trump his earned victory on National TV at a time when Trump was looking for all the help he could get. Thanks a lot smiling Tucker.

The audience reaction ought to wipe away that cocky smile. It could not have come at a worse time as we were trying to figure who was for us and who was against us. Fox and Tucker Carlson were the big losers in my personal search.

Those weren't the insults reserved for a CNN or MSNBC anchor on Friday. No, *Traitor, Globalist, and Sellout* were the insults aimed at our one-time conservative media darling Tucker Carlson. In what feels like the most severe moment of backlash since his Fox News show premiered in 2016, Carlson rightfully has been dealing with criticism from guys like me on the right.

[BTW, as of late near the end of January, my friends tell me Tucker seems to have mended his ways. Trust is a hard thing to win back. Let me continue my assault on Tucker because I don't think I'll ever be back to FOX like I once was.]

It was well over a month ago on a Thursday that Carlson angered most of his audience when he called out Sidney Powell, President Trump's attorney who has peddled the truth about the Democratic conspiracy to steal the election. Tucker did not deviate too far from the Dem party line, opening his show with deference to the fraud claims presented by Rudy Giuliani.

That's what made him hard to figure out at first. He also offered up reasons his audience should trust him. He explained to his viewers that he had reached out to Powell for supporting evidence with an open mind. And he pointed out his coverage of the Russia probe and how he never rules anything out — even UFOs. He knew he was wrong and we were all looking for some support, not controversy.

Tucker eventually broke the news ever so softly to his viewers: He said that, despite his polite requests, Powell had not provided a shred of evidence to support her *outlandish* claims and had even told him to stop contacting her. He pretended to be hurt. Once he called her work outlandish he was finished by me. You sold us out Tucker.

How is it that I never wavered from Sidney and I do not have the facts that a huge network like Fox can provide. Fox abandoned Trump and Tucker Carlson followed. Former President Trump noticed and he railed against FOX til the day he flew to Mara Largo on AF1 for the last time. FOX lost a good part of its audience and an apology would be nice from R. Murdoch.

After weeks of showing evidence to everybody she could, Carlson claimed that Sidney Powell had failed to provide him with evidence, and she had also failed to support her claims to others in Trump World. He is full of himself. She showed more than she had to show to an arrogant Carlson. I saw it. Too bad that Tucker lied.

Tucker Carlson is simply a Traitor, Globalist, and a Sellout I am not letting him off the hook so easily. He created a controversy for his ratings. He deserves no accolades for his diatribe against Trump that he made off as if it was against Sidney Powell. No apology! Sorry Tucker. Good-bye.

Pro-Trump internet personalities have criticized good ole Tucker for having the nerve to challenge Powell. Humph! I don't think so. Tucker Carlson was "insulting" and "rude." What was Sidney's sin? Support for Trump? Sorry Tucker – hope you learned your lesson.

Tucker Carlson the consummate skeptic

"What Powell was describing would amount to the single greatest crime in American history," Carlson told his legions of viewers. "Millions of votes stolen in a day. Democracy destroyed…We invited Sidney Powell on the show. We would have given her the whole hour. We would have given her the entire week actually . . . But she never sent us any evidence despite requests, polite requests. When we kept pressing she got angry and told us to stop contacting her."

Tucker, you are either for Trump or against him. What do you think the stolen election is—a joke-- that you can manipulate to get higher ratings by attacking a major Trump supporter. I see you clearly my boy! Call it a day my boy! You are done with me.

Tucker Eliminatus!

Chapter 6 Georgia Is a Double Battleground State

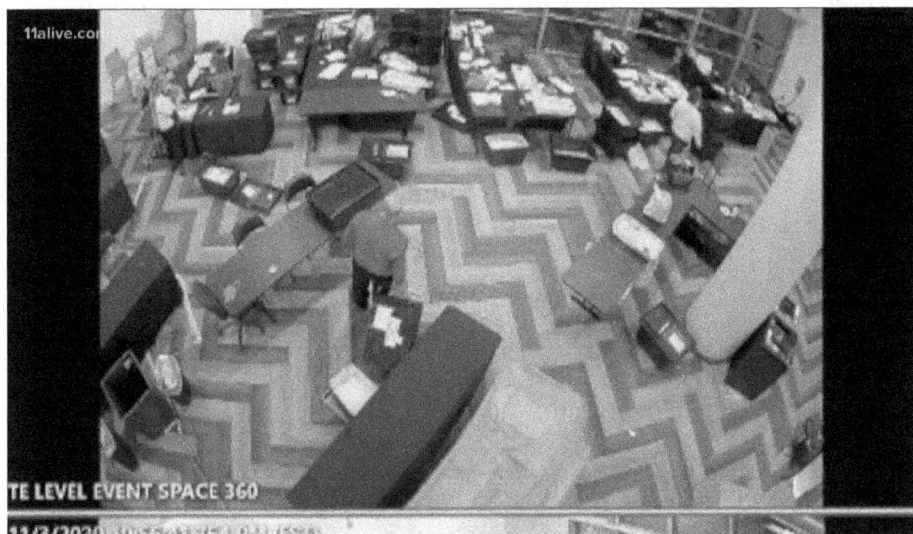

The Committee on Government Oversight in Georgia has general jurisdiction over state government programs and policies. Senator Bill Heath is Chairman. Marty Harbin is Vice Chairman.

The Georgia Senate conducted major hearings following persistent accusations among supporters of President Donald Trump and those Democrats simply trying to assure elections are conducted fairly in America. The cry was that all legal American votes should be counted and illegal votes cast aside.

Some Georgia state leaders have repeatedly rejected claims of issues in conducting the elections claiming there is no evidence of widespread fraud or any kind of concerted effort to manipulate Georgia's results. Yet, after the hearings it is now clear that something is dreadfully wrong in Georgia.

Georgia Sen. Jeff Mullis is one of many state senators who supported the Senate Government Oversight and Judiciary Subcommittee Hearings that first took place Thursday, December 3rd.

"Due to a number of alleged discrepancies brought to the legislature's attention following the general election, I believe a thorough and robust review of our election procedures is necessary to avoid similar issues in the future," said Sen. Mullis. "I believe these hearings will shed some light on potential inefficiencies in our elections system and highlight areas of possible future improvement. I plan on introducing legislation during the upcoming legislative session with the intent of improving our current elections process and ensuring that only legal votes are cast and counted."

Here are a few comments from the end of a web article on the Georgia Hearings. Somehow no matter what SCOTUS rounds in favor of the Democrats.

There are hordes of evidence of election fraud, malfeasance etc. However, the media and the Dems with some RINO assist, deny it exists at all. And that's all it takes, in this political/social atmosphere, combined with media blackout, to put Biden in the White House.

If the Fulton County Board of Elections will not allow "the forensic examination to be conducted," then an armed militia unit needs to immediately confront the Board… and – at whatever cost – insure that the examination does indeed occur. All future elections, nationwide, depend upon it.

SCOTUS (CJ: John Roberts) has already rejected the Texas suit, which was valid, as there WAS standing, because there was provable damages. All legitimate votes were affected by the fraudulently obtained outcome. Even a Chief Justice can be removed from office (unless we enter a feudal state).

It seems that the majority of government department heads, and way too many politicians are fighting to protect the system they thrive in. And America, both its heritage and its future, be damned.

On December 30 at another hearing by the same group, there were real fireworks in Georgia

https://www.ammoland.com/2020/12/expert-testimony-by-jovan-hutton-pulitzer-at-georgia-ballot-hearing-is-devastating/#ixzz6iWC1pYOj

Under Creative Commons License: Attribution
Follow us: @Ammoland on Twitter | Ammoland on Facebook

You won't regret reading the following:

The Georgia Senate has taken the election discrepancies seriously. After grouping to hold hearings a month after the elections, they really got their act together on the day before New Year's Eve with a slew of expert witnesses. Here I am today January 24, recounting what might have been while Democrats are preparing their articles of impeachment to present to a new US Senate tomorrow Monday 1/25/2021.

The person in these hearings that I was impressed with the most is a gentleman named Jovann Hutton Pulitzer. I spent 23 plus years as an IBM Senior Systems Engineer helping explain technical matters to a ton of clients and fellow IBMers.

I was and still am deeply impressed with Pulitzer and the SCOTUS should have also been impressed. If I heard Pulitzer, this election was so important, the SCOTUS should have also heard him. They work for America and Americans—supposedly anyway. But, they do not care, leading calls for their dismissal.

He may not be especially likable but Mr. Pulitzer is a true expert in scanning technology and his work is responsible for the scanning software on all our cell phones. He has over 200 patents and his experience gives him the ability to tell a fake ballot from a real one. He made his expertise known on December 30 and elicited a ton of questions from the Senators. I saw his complete presentation Wow! Did SCOTUS see Pulitzer in action. I doubt it. They did not care enough to protect America from rogue Democrats who committed a major fraud.

U.S.A. —(AmmoLand.com)-

"On December 30, 2020, Jovan Hutton Pulitzer gave a presentation to the Georgia State Senate Judiciary Subcommittee, on how he and his company can detect many types of election fraud with a simple, easy examination of the physical ballots. His approach did not rely on eye-balling ballots and trying to discern things that to the human eye are indiscernible.

Pulitzer said his company machines simply run the ballots through specially designed forensic machines. Their functional design is for them to be able to detect the physical signatures of the ballots.

Pulitzer is a pattern recognition expert holding over 200 patents." He said he could find all the fraudulent ballots that would never be found by eye. Somebody had to give him a chance. Too bad US officials are all dinkers and would rather trust the corrupt Demo**rats**.

Dr. Pulitzer is quite the expert. His patents are used on 12 billion handheld devices around the world." He is as impressive in person as his technology credentials are magnanimous.

His point in his presentation is that nobody should care about handwritten signatures. It is a guessing game to verify them. Machine audited ballots are 100% accurate. He told the Senators "machs nichts." The signatures are not on the ballots.

Pulitzer gave an enlightening presentation showing how the physical nature of a ballot changes over time from when it is sent out, signed, returned scanned, etc. Each time his analysis shows that the ballot signature appears differently to the scanner. The trail of ballot signatures can be used to definitely identify fraudulent ballots. But some officials including the SCOTUS should care enough about the Country to check these things out well. But they do not see their role as important in national issues If so, SCOTUS< please step down because there are those of us who agree to pay you because we think that is your purpose.

Clearly if Georgia or any state wanted to prove or disprove fraud, they would use the method Dr. Pulitzer prescribed so well. He demonstrated how his methods would-be able to detect at a 100% rate the physical signatures of folding, printing, marking and codes that exist on the paper used for the ballot What Senator can do that with his or her eyeballs?

He convinced the Senators that every physical process done to a ballot leaves a specific identifiable mark. The marks describe the ballots legitimate or illegitimate journey to the machine. Those minuscule marks, often invisible to the human eye, are the physical signatures Mr. Pulitzer talks about.

A Pulitzer style physical forensic audit of the paper ballots would completely circumvent the election software. In other words, it could tell a story without needing the Dominion machine or the Dominion software. Why did Georgia not want to know? Why did the SCOTUS pretend they did not know?

Here's how the Pulitzer technique finds bad ballots and assures good ballots:

1. His method examines the folds on the paper ballot.
2. At the beginning of the process, these ballots were folded by machine, and each valid one was folded identically.
3. Pulitzer can post facto run the ballots through a device, and it will spit out every ballot that was not folded by an official machine.
4. If they slipped fake ballots in, his system would pick it up at once. No human eyeballs are required.

Mr. Pulitzer gave a great presentation and he answered questions afterward. The following is one of his best answers. He discussed how his process can tell you, with 100% accuracy:

• How many ballots were printed by what machine.
• How many ballots were mailed.

- How many ballots were filled out by machine.
- How many ballots were counted more than once.
- How many ballots were scanned more than once.
- What candidates were marked on all the ballots in the categories above.
- What ballots went through adjudication

Why would Democrats say no? Because the election handler's default was to simply award Biden the victory regardless of whether there was an issue or provable fraud. I think the SCOTUS was incompetent and uncaring and irreverent in closing down the appeals and the original jurisdiction disputes. I wish I knew why they favored a Biden presidency because for what they knew, they assured it.

CJ John Roberts instructed the other Supremes to doom America because he was afraid of ANTIFA and BLM visiting his own home. SNOPES says that is not true. SNOPES is an instrument of the left. We all know that. So, all of America now has a corrupt Joe Biden family in office and unless we are tough against them, he will be untouchable for the next four years. Surely Roberts could have asked for 26,000 National Guard troops to protect SCOTUS if he had the guts. He was not comfortable enough to do his job properly.

One of the Biden slides that is damaging to the validity of his election in Mr. Pulitzer's presentation shows a quote from a Fulton County Election official, saying 106,000 of 113,130 votes were adjudicated (hand verified). In other words, the voting machine software could not determine to whom the ballot was cast.

Pulitzer noted that a state does not need voting machines when they do not work? Pulitzer said this was a signal for the person who bought the machines to stop using them and to get the people's money back. If the machines can't accurately count the ballots then all ballots should be counted by hand, don't you think?

What should this mean to the average joe. Nothing! However, this means that the percentage needing human intervention to determine the ballot was an astounding 93.67% adjudication rate. The machine could not do the job paid for in 93.67% of the ballots. So what happened then? So called human "experts" in the county had to guess the intent of the voter. Somehow these votes were almost always adjudicated in Biden's favor. It's the luck of the Irish I suppose. How did Biden get all the votes that humans had determined. Were the humans Democrats. Oh, yes they were but they were honest????

We're talking about dots on pieces of paper so how would a human be able to tell better than a machine unless the machine were rigged to send the ballot to a human. . Well, the expert says the machine was broken (or rigged) and should have been taken offline and replaced with a machine that worked.

Check out acceptable rates of rejection. Typical rates and rates in the past in Georgia for example were in the neighborhood of 1% to 2% -- not 90% and certainly not 93% and certainly not 93.67%. If it were not fraud, how would this happen? Did the SCOTUS tell us this answer in their decision not to decide?

What would be the norm? A 2% reading would be high. Pulitzer told the Senators that the high adjudication rate shows the machines were not working as they should have been and the machines should have been replaced before finishing their job. Georgia election officials were seemingly pleased with being able to adjudicate by hand.

Was the SCOTUS interested enough in the truth to save the election against fraud? The people overwhelming believe   No sir or mam. Scotus led by John Roberts were concerned more about living the next day because they had not asked for 26,000 troops to guard their homes. SCOTUS Eliminatus

The machines were not doing the job as they had promised. Dr. Pulitzer said that the Georgia rate shows similarities with high adjudication rates in Michigan and Nevada; two other states that if the continued search for the truth were permitted would have been proven that the party in charge of the machines had attempted one way or another to steal the election for Vice President Biden. DID SCOTUS care? Not that I could see.

Was it an accident? If it were an accident why did everything (all votes) adjudicate to Mr. Biden's favor. Was there a steal in play? Of course the steal was on. Republican wimps and the wimps in

SCOTUS chose to give the Trump election to Joe Biden. The Democrats expected no less.

Georgia officials had been talking about how difficult it would be to check the ballot signatures. Not so if they used the Pulitzer process, which he offered the state for free. Mr. Pulitzer in fact answered a Senator's question by saying that his process can do the forensic analysis quickly and cheaply for all paper ballots. It never happened, unfortunately for the country.

In fact, he promised to do the work for free for Georgia to prove that their election was very inaccurate. He did not need the money as his patents give him enough money to live well without ever working another day in his life. Check me out!

Let me repeat that. Mr. Pulitzer volunteered his company for free to the Senators to do the forensic evaluation of the paper ballots *for free.* He has donated his time, expertise, equipment, and company assets.

There is a man who cares. I wish you could have seen his presentation. The SCOTUS should love America only half as much as I. But they do not!

Pulitzer says he does not care who wins. His game was to help America stop a bad Democratic game of ballot stealing. He simply wanted to ensure that an accurate count was made, so this time could be adjudicated by the people properly and the next time, this could never happen again.

Pulitzer says, without faith in the election process, we do not have a country. How does the SCOTUS feel about that comment? Mr. Roberts, speak to the press and tell them I am wrong on you if you can. But, you cannot!

While Jovan Hutton Pulitzer was giving his testimony to the subcommittee, more information came in. Voting was ongoing in the runoff elections for Senators in Georgia. There is a Twitter video of what Pulitzer had to report.

Twitter link about ability to hack into the Georgia machines live.

Was Pulitzer able to hack into the DOMINION machines in Georgia live?

WE ARE IN.

"At this very moment at a polling location in the county, *NOT ONLY* do we now have access through the devices to the POLL PAD, to the system, but *WE ARE IN.*"

Georgia hearing reveals LIVE, real-time hacking of Dominion Voting… Here is a partial transcript of what Pulitzer reported at that time:

"At this very moment, at a polling locating in the County, not only do we now have access to the devices, to the poll pad, the system, but we are in. And it is not supposed to have WIFI, and that is not supposed to be able to happen, so we've documented now, its communicating two ways, in real time, mean it is receiving data and sending data, should never happen, shouldn't be WIFI, we've now documented it in real time, so we can shut down the data. But that is going on right there where everyone is voting. And, I just wanted to get it into the record."

The subcommittee was impressed with Mr. Pulitzer's testimony. They voted to request that the Fulton County Board of elections allow examination of the paper ballots. This is a transcript of the request/resolution of the subcommittee:

"That the Fulton County Board of Elections would make the absentee ballots cast in Fulton County, on the November 3 election, before the November 3rd election, be made available to be inspected by the Chealy Group, through the process that Mr. Pulitzer outlined earlier today."

The vote was unanimous and affirmative.

The Georgia State Senate Judiciary Subcommittee does not control any police. It is not clear that if more votes by the full committee or the Senate are required. It is not clear if the Fulton County Board of Elections will allow the forensic examination to be conducted.

I suspect we would have had two different Senators if the truth were permitted. It can all be blamed of a SCOTUS that did not give two craps about America. SCOTUS Eliminatus.

SCOTUS, the Court that says the truth really does not matter is we the Supremes choose not to hear the case. Dear SCOTUS, consider yourselves eliminated in the minds of other Americans. SCOTUS Eliminatus!

The methods portrayed by Mr. Pulitzer are convincing. They offer a simple way to detect several different kinds of election tampering. They are not absolute. They would not detect, for example, double voting with fraudulently obtained ballots, phantom voting, or voting by illegal voters. However, they would do much to restore confidence in the election process. Not hearing a case to help America is a legacy of this Supreme Court. SCOTUS Eliminatus.

Will the Fulton County Board of Elections fight this attempt to show transparency in the election process?

If past history is any indicator, this group of officials will lawyer up and create legal excuses not to allow the examination. They appear to be crooked but they may just be convinced by ignorance that they

are right in their obstinance. Not allowing the examination, however, does make them appear to be guilty. They do not seem to care. They think the windage is on their side, whatever that means,
Because of all this stupidity, America has the wrong president for the next four years. I sure hope a lot of people are in jail for more than four years as we cannot give them another four years to make their attacks undetectable.

Chapter 7 President Trump's Nov 4 Georgia Rally

Here are some facts that I gleaned from President Trump's Rally on January 4 for the two Georgia Senate Candidate. Unfortunately even for the Georgia Runoff, the Dem / progressive steal was on and both "conservative" candidates lost. The SCOTUS could have easily prevented this if they had opted to do the right thing. If the Trump lawsuits had prevailed both candidates would have won without this illegitimate and what would have been an unneeded runoff. Now America has Joe Biden. I rest my case.

With full Trump support, both Georgia candidates would have survived without a runoff. Moreover, the two R Senators would be in the Congress today. President Biden would be a little more careful flaunting his power, and America could rest a little easier about having 103 Supreme Court Justices and having no filibuster. Besides, Americans would have no concern about Washington DC and Puerto Rico as new states with four US Senators between them.

Hawaii and Alaska our last two states chose not to weigh in on the potential controversy. But, they are very liberal progressive in nature and we know where their hearts are. Watch the impeachment coming up and you will see RINO Murkowski in action and you may wish Alaska had not been granted Statehood.

Regarding Georgia, if SCOTUS had taken the Texas case, which was slam dunk if it were heard and adjudicated fairly, Georgia would not have had a runoff election on January 5. But, CJ John Roberts has no scruples as a conservative and he ordered the other justices to protect his lily livered butt as he screamed through the chamber walls for the other SCOTUS associate justices to forget about doing what was best for America.

Chief Justice Roberts was afraid and so he ordered the others to protect their own butts from becoming victimized by riots from ANTIFA and BLM and other radicals supporting the Democrats and Joe Biden. Roberts more or less ordered the other justices to stand down and not vote to hear the biggest case that would ever reach them or any other SCOTUS—ever, ever and ever again. The SCOTUS is hereby declared a stagnant piece of guano, not worthy of the tailoring job cost on their fancy robes.

Nonetheless, corrupt justice Roberts had his way with his underlings. And thus the call from the people for SCOTUS Eliminatus. I am only the spokesperson for the cause. The SCOTUS knows nobody alive in late 2020-early 2021 loves it or even likes it anymore. So, why not just resign.

It is a truism that you can only cheat the people a few times before they all realize it is your sorry butt that you care about and not theirs.

Once the SCOTUS had punted and the runoff was on, it was time to win it. Trump helped all he could but the people felt the R candidates in Georgia were not clean. Where were they rallying for Trump when he needed it? The people like me said to themselves, why when the two candidates did not do all they could to prove the illegitimacy in GA of the Trump election should we back them wholeheartedly. And, so they lost but the fraud probably was the major reason. Nobody had stamped it out.

Trump campaigned hard for the Georgia-Two but he was clearly annoyed that they were not so out in front of the deal with him. These two seemed to feel impervious to an R / conservative backlash. Yet, they got it and now neither carries the title "Senator."

They got the backlash for their inaction for sure but in addition to that, they got to feel the pain of a rigged Georgia election. Had they made a fuss over the election rigged v Trump, they would have had more standing in why they lost their own elections.

From my perspective, they did not help Trump and if they had, they would have won. If Trump succeeded in his challenges, it would have helped them also. They played both sides against the middle and they figured even without the Prez, they could survive. But it did not happen that way. They appeared luke-warm for Trump and the people did not come out and vote when it was just them after Trump had lost.

They had nobody working for them who could have had their own Senate elections determined valid. They would have won on the trump challenges but not on their won.

As I see it, once these RINOS from Georgia apparently accepted that Trump had lost, the voters no longer cared about them. If a squirrel or a groundhog ran against them, they would have won as Dem candidates. The people know their friends. Unfortunately a squirrel or a groundhog interpreter was not able to be located in time for campaign speeches. We reap what we sew!

President Trump thought as most Republicans and conservatives thought that Mike Pence, Trump's one-time loyal VP would come through for the American people on January 6, the day after the runoff election.. Trump said a few things at the rally about how he was counting on Pence. Pence screwed Trump up against a stone wall.

> "We're not gonna let it happen over the past. And I hope Mike Pence comes through for us, I have to tell you. I hope that our great Vice-President, our great Vice-President comes through for us. He's a great guy. Of course, if he doesn't come through, I won't like him quite as much. No, Mike is a great guy.
>
> He's a, he's a wonderful man and a smart man, and a man that I like a lot, but he's gonna have a lot to say about it, and he -- You know, one thing with him, you're gonna get straight shots. He's gonna call it straight. Over the past few weeks, we've demonstrated that we won the election in a landslide.

I had once thought it would be OK if something bad happened to Donald Trump—not a stolen election—that Mike Pence would be a good president. No longer. Pence stabbed Trump in the back and he deserves nothing to eat for life other than the hot dogs that Satan can make him in hell No, I am not kidding.

What do I mean? A weak Mike Pence, and then Mitch McConnell both took their daggers out and put them through Trump's heart and the collective heart of conservative America. They better not have political aspirations because for guys like me, they are finished.

Trump knows that more than 75 million people voted for him. My guess is the real number is between 85 million and 90 million as Trump votes were shaved for Biden's gain by Dominion voting machines. Yes, I said that. In fact if you count the Dominion switched votes to Biden, it was probably more like 85 or 90 million. And Biden would be lucky of he got 65 million.

Either way, it was the most of any incumbent president in the history of our country. Using the 75 million number, Trump won over 11 million compared to his last outing It was close to 12 million more votes than 2016, one of the largest. It was actually the single largest increase in the history of our country. No person that won, went to a second term or went through an election where he got nearly 12 million more votes. Nonetheless the SCOTUS could not be bothered with doing their paid jobs of adjudication of disputes in America.

Trump added great comments at GA Rally:

No, it never happened before, never happened before. We made historic gains among African-Americans, Hispanic-Americans, Asian-Americans, and we won the largest share of non-white vote of any Republican president in 60 years. We also won 18 out of 19 bellwether counties. Now when you win just a few bellwether counties, you always win the election.

Tonight our mission here in Georgia is to make sure the radical left cannot rob you of your voice and your votes in Washington. You can't lose -- these two people, and I really know them well. They're the most respected people. They're great people and they really do have a voice, and they love their state and they love their country.

The continuation of the steal caused both to lose their first round without a recount.

The Democrats have been trying to steal the White House for four years before the. November 3 election. Through hook and crook, they were seemingly successful this time except the people don't believe it. Trump exclaimed that we could not let them. You just can't let them -- steal the U.S. Senate.

You can't let it happen. You can't let it happen. He noted that David and Kelly were running against the most extreme liberal candidates in the history of Georgia, probably in the history of our country. He was talking about Jon Ossoff and Raphael Warnock. Despite all the rally hoopla, the Democrats stole this election too. What the heck, they have cheating down to a "science."

At the rally, President Trump went through the mechanics of the steal. It is hard for realists on the election not to cry:

> We were up 293,000 votes in Michigan. 112,000 votes in Washington. In Wisconsin. We were way up. 356,000 votes in Georgia. 356,000. And 700,000 votes in Pennsylvania. It was -- over. I should've run up to the podium and said, "Thank you very much for this wonderful victory." Then maybe they wouldn't have had time to close those booths, right? The counting rooms. And do what they did. But then it all started to disappear. Since the election, we have put forth indisputable evidence documenting the rampant fraud, which will be announced on Wednesday, as you know.

...

> And we were leading all of them by a lot until, like a miracle, it started to quickly disappear. Right here in Georgia there were tens of thousands of illegal votes cast and counted. You know that. And here are just a few examples. Watch this bit tomorrow [for the GA runoff election]. We're up 10,315. Ballots were cast by individuals whose name and date of birth matches a Georgia resident who died in 2020 prior to the election and your wacky Secretary of State said, "two people. "Two people and the Governor."

Who knows

> How many people are on that list, but it's a lot of people. 205,006 ballots were cast -- Why individuals whose name and date of birth matches an incarcerated felon in a Georgia prison? Maybe they aren't all there, but they did a lot of work… 4502 illegal ballots were cast by individuals who do not appear on the state's voter rolls.

Well, that's sort of strange. 18,325 illegal ballots were cast by individuals who registered to vote using an address listed as vacant according to the Postal Service. At least 86,880 ballots were cast by people whose registrations were illegally backdated. Oh, I can't believe that happened. 66,000 votes -- You all have to understand, we're down by a little more than 11,000, so every one of these is determinative. 66,000 votes in Georgia were cast by people under the legal voting age.

At least 15,000 ballots were cast by individuals who moved out of this state prior to the November 3rd election. Now, maybe they moved back in. I don't know. I mean, I can't tell. They moved out. Ah, let's go back. Usually, it takes a little time, right? You know. We moved out. Let's go back, darling. Georgia's absentee ballot rejection rate went from an average of 3% in 2016 and then went down very low to almost zero.

Now, ah, think of it. Almost zero. If you multiply that out, and this is with many, many more ballots pouring in, went to almost zero. 48 out of 159 counties in Georgia rejected no ballots at all. These absentee ballot rejection rates prove that the tens of thousands of illegitimate ballots were counted.

There were more absentee ballots in 2020 than ever before by far, but magically, far fewer ballots were rejected. This alone is more than enough to swing the election to us. This one thing. I'm going over individual, in all of the swing states. Now, they'll check this out, and that's fine, and, but you take a look at it.

Officials egregiously violated state laws in order to solicit, facilitate, and promote cheating and theft on a scale never seen before. These crooked and incompetent officials suspended signature verification. I said, "I want you to go to Fulton County to check the signatures because hundreds of thousands of ballots came in.

I want you to check the signature to see if it compares to somebody that lived there two years, four years, or six years ago." They don't want to do it. The Secretary of State and your incompetent governor, although he thinks I've been a great president. They illegally flooded their states with absentee ballots, and they deployed hundreds of illicit ballot drop boxes in corrupt Democrat-run cities, among many other flagrant violations of law.

They put these drop-boxes there, and in a number of cases, they'd be gone for three days. They'd take them up, and they'd, where are they? Where are they? They were gone. Georgia's secretary of state agreed to a litigation settlement, which is something that nobody's ever seen one like this. I want, I want to just tell you that Stacey Abrams took him to the cleaners.

That drastically and illegally changed the state's election procedures. They never got the mandated approval from your state legislature, who by the way, you have some great people in your legislature, some great, great people who agree with what we're saying, and even more so. But think of it. They never got the approval.

President Trump reminded the onlookers of how it is supposed to work. By law, he said, under the US Constitution, you can't just do these deals and not get the approval. It is not OK! And your secretary of state, or whoever it was, made this horrible consent decree [with Stacie Abrams}. This got rid of so much safety. The president referred to what happened as "a disgraceful thing." And it was only approved by your local, uh, politicians, not the state legislatures.

SCOTUS of course kept their noses clean. Why would they enter a fray so important to the American people? John Roberts told them that ANTIFA and BLM would be rioting in front of the associate justice's homes if they took up a case to help Trump. These cowards disappointed a lot of Americans I'd say about 85 million to 90 million citizens who actually voted for Trump are not pleased. SCOTUS could have put this to bed but opted the scaredy-cat way out. Donald Trump urged Pence to do the right thing but Pence pulled a Jeff Sessions on him.

Consider that nobody told the Democrats in at least ten states that they had the authority to cheat and steal the election. Pence failed to act because he was not sure he had the authority. SCOTUS and Pence wimped out. Trump was right. If Pence had assumed he had the authority to have the states resubmit their electors, the outcome would have changed to Trump's favor.

The SOCTUS was well aware that the State Legislators Had been begging Pence to send the delegates home for a redo. Pence was not a strong enough person to do what was right. Democrats were strong enough to cheat and steal in broad daylight and having authority was not an issue for them. Here is what Trump asked Pence:

"If Mike Pence does the right thing we win the election," Trump told thousands of supporters who rallied Wednesday on the Ellipse, just south of the White House, an hour before the count in Congress was to begin.

"All Vice President Pence has to do is send it back to the states to recertify and we become president and you are the happiest people," Trump said, repeating a falsehood he has been promoting leading up to the congressional session.

Trump repeatedly pressured Pence to act during his more than 75-minute speech to supporters. "Mike Pence is going to have to come through for us," Trump said, "and if he doesn't, it's a sad day for our country."

Well folks, Mike Pence did not have the guts to assume authority to overcome the Democrats illegitimate steal and power grab. Dems took Pence's authority and mocked it.

Mike Pence followed the coward's lead from SCOTUS. He could have put the issue to bed by sending the determinations back to the state legislatures and not approve the submitted illegitimate electors. He was afraid that he did not have the power. The whole country depended on Pence. Trump depended on Pence. You and I depended on Pence and the SCOTUS. We were sadly disappointed. Trump added the following truisms;

And local judges. You can't do that. You have to have your state legislatures do it. That's true with all states. Tens of thousands of votes are missing. We go all over the world telling people how to run their elections, and we don't even know how to run ours. The most unhappy person right now anywhere in the United States is Hillary Clinton because she's asking -- The Democrat Party, why the hell didn't you do this for me? [Audience chants "Lock her up"] True.

Why didn't you do it for me? Why the hell didn't you -- You notice how quiet she's been? I shouldn't have said that. Now tonight, she'll -- But you notice how quiet? She's furious because she said, "Don't forget. I won Michigan by 10,000 votes." We did much better, as I said, this time. Much, much better.

But I won Michigan from her by 10,000 votes. I won Wisconsin by a small -- You know? I mean, they could've done that one and not get caught. We caught 'em. We caught 'em. And I say to people like Mike Lee that are here and Lindsey. I say if they got approved and verified, they used the word verified, votes that are fraudulent, and then we find out after because you can't do it that quickly.

It doesn't go that quickly. It's a lot of work and a lot of votes and a lot of people. And then we find out that there were frauds. Like in one state where you had let's say you lost by 25,000 votes, they verify it, and that's supposed to be the end. But shortly thereafter, we find out that we actually won the state by 250,000 votes.

… The president recounted that In Wisconsin, over 90,000 ballots were illegally harvested. You just cannot do that. You are not allowed to. It was effected by these so-called human drop boxes.

And over 500 illegal unmanned drop boxes were put out statewide. In addition, over 170,000 absentee votes were counted that are blatantly illegal under Wisconsin law and should never have been included in the tally. By the way, I lost. It -- it was razor thin. There's 170,000 votes. The margin in Wisconsin is only 20,000 votes, so this issue alone would've won that state for us many times over.

We were leading at 10:00 in the evening by a lot. In Pennsylvania, there were 205,000 more ballots cast than there were voters. How do you get around that [Inaudible]? Which remains completely unexplained. You have great senators and representatives there and nobody can explain it. But think of that. And in other places too.

You had more ballots than you had voters. You had more votes, think of it, than you had voters by a lot. In addition, Democrat State Supreme Court judges and Democrat Secretary of State effectively abolished the signature verification process right here. They counted ballots cast after deadlines and they allowed ballots to be illegally fixed in Democrat-controlled areas.

Another point of fact is that there is an unexplained 400,000 vote discrepancy between the number of mail-in ballots in Pennsylvania sent out reported on November 2nd, 2020 and the number reported on November 4th. They can't explain it. 400,000 previously unreported mail-in ballots magically appeared. The officials could not explain it. And all of a sudden they just happened to find 400,000. President Trump commented:

That's a lot of people. Amazing. And the Pennsylvania Legislature is not happy. Pennsylvania also had an estimated 8,000 dead voters, 55,000 ballots received back before they were even sent. How about that? The ballots were received but they weren't sent yet. "Oh, uh, get 'em out fast, please." Many more with no mail date and 14,000 ballots illegally cast by out-of-state voters.

Those are numbers and those are numbers we got from them so they can't say, "Oh, the numbers aren't so good." In Clark County, Nevada, over 130,000 ballots -- This is far -- Just so you know all these numbers, these are far more than we need, were processed on machines where the signature matching threshold was intentionally lowered to a level that you could sign your name Santa Claus and it wouldn't pick it up.

Didn't pick up anything. More than 42,000 people in Nevada double voted. That's more than we needed by far. In Arizona more than 36,000 votes were cast by non-citizens. And there were 11,000 more ballots than there were voters. Seems to be a trait, doesn't it? This was like at the Super Bowl where you have 15 cameras and they say, "Camera number 4, you're on.

In Michigan, according to one analyst, over 35,000 ballots listed no address. Over 13 ballots were cast by non-residents, and an estimated 17,000 ballots were cast by dead people. Some dead people, by the way, also requested an application. It's true. Those are the ones that really bother me.

They not only vote, but they request an application, that's a double. In addition, there is the highly troubling matter of Dominion voting machines. And I want you to watch this very carefully tomorrow, everybody. You have to watch it carefully. I want to read you from a letter from Georgia State Senator William Ligon.

A highly respected official, Senator Ligon wrote: . "Dear Mr. President: As Chairman of the Georgia Senate Judiciary Committee on Elections, I request that you immediately send an outside team of cyber experts to investigate potential hacking and other irregularities associated with Dominion Voting Systems scanners, ballot marking devices, ballot's, polling pads used in the 2020 General Election in Georgia."

The President complained that you don't hear this from your Georgia Secretary of State and you don't hear this from your Governor He added:

And you do have a great legislature, I have to tell you. But the Governor won't let them hold a session to de-certify. "On December 30, 2020 the committee held a hearing investigating potential fraud and other irregularities during Georgia's 2020 General Election. The committee first unanimously approved a report dated December 17, 2020 discussing a myriad of voting irregularities and potential fraud in Georgia 2020 General Election discussed in an earlier hearing held on December 3. Notably, the committee stated in the executive summary that the November 3rd, 2020, General Election was chaotic and reported results must be viewed as untrustworthy." They are untrustworthy, despite the line of crap that you hear from these people that represent you.

I don't know where they come from? "The committee then heard," and this is from one of your most highly respected political representatives, "The committee then heard additional testimony concerning voting irregularities during the 2020 General Election including testimony and a real-time test demonstrating serious irregularities with Dominion's voting machines.

Three events discussed at this hearing stand out and require a forensic order of the Dominion voting machines in Georgia to be immediately conducted." The Governor will not let us do it. We've been asking him now since November 4th, the day after the election. He won't let us do it. Why won't he let us do it?

There's only one reason I can think of. First, the Dominion voting machines employed in Fulton County," that's the home of Stacey had an astounding 93.67 error rate. Ninety-three point six seven error rate in the scanning of ballots requiring a review panel to adjudicate or determine the voter's intent." So they're going to a voter intent, "What did the voter mean by this vote?" Somebody votes for Trump, "Ah, you know, I think that voter meant something other.

He doesn't want Trump, let's just switch it around." Think of that, they're trying to determine the voter's intent in over 106,000 ballots out of a total of 113,000 ballots. This is from your representative, highly respected, "The national average for such an error rate is far less than 1.2%," so that was 93%. "The source of this astronomical error rate must be identified to determine if these machines were set up or designated to allow for a third party to disregard the actual ballot cast by the registered voter." This is what I have.

This guy's sitting there -- "Well, can you connect into the machines?" "Yes." "How do you do that?" Within about 25 seconds he controlled the internet. Former Vice President Biden led Georgia by only 11,779 votes. Every one of the things I told you about, almost, is more votes than what we're talking about.

The crime that was committed in this state is immeasurable. An immediate forensic audit of an appropriate sampling of Dominion's voting machines and related equipment is critical to determine the level of illegal fraudulent ballots improperly counted in Georgia during the 2020 General Election, and during tomorrow's race.

The president read another letter

Let me also quickly read a letter from Mark Finchem, chairman of the Arizona House -- a very respected man -- Federal Relations Committee. "Dear Mister President, Subsequent to the election, members of the legislature were inundated with complaints from constituents relating to the intensity of the General Election, and the integrity" -- More important than anything else -- "And the accuracy of canvased results.

in many instances, constituents reported that their earlier in-person ballots may not have been correctly processed or tabulated by Maricopa County officials. Members of the legislature have conducted two public hearings in recent weeks, during which significant evidence of fraudulent and illegal voting in Arizona has been demonstrated, through expert and eyewitness testimony." For example in Pima County, and Maricopa County, it appears that 143,000 illegal votes were actually injected into the ballot system.

The president made a great speech from his heart. The election clearly was stolen. Mitch McConnell and the other Republican RINOS should not be given the opportunity to represent conservatives ever again.

Think of that! No, but think of this. Also, and, I, I, -- you know, the press wont report this. They're probably turning off -- "Oh, we don't like this." They don't like this. They don't want to talk about numbers. They talked about my phone call. They don't like my phone call. Everyone loved my phone call.

They don't like talking about numbers, because nobody knew the numbers were so egregious. Also, an expert mathematician concluded that the only explanation for the actual voting results in Arizona is that 100%, think of this, 130% of democrats voted for candidate Biden. And a negative 30% voted for President Trump.

Now, think of that. In order to get to the numbers, 130% of the voters -- that's a little tough to get, okay? -- had to vote for him; and minus 30 had to vote for me. And that gets you to 100% and nobody has 100% voting. For all of these people who think it's too late Does that mean that we're forced to approve a fraudulent election or an election with massive irregularities.

Why don't our politicians care?

Worse than all of that, there is one group of people who are paid to care. Their name is The Supreme Court of the United States of America. We call them SCOTUS which is that big long title and we just assume the "of America" part. They did not do their job. They let us down.

They knew the People were cheated and they stood by idly and just let it happen. We do not need a Supreme Court that opts out of the most important decision ever given to a United States Court and perhaps since America is the strongest country in the world, this was the most important decision in world history and these wimps abdicated their responsibility. They did not do their jobs. They should all be fired.   Check out the next chapter

Chapter 8 Summary of Dr. Navarro's 1st Election Report

Navarro Report – The Immaculate Deception

Even if Americans who perhaps have or have not paid attention to the mechanics of the Democrat's steal, do not agree in total, there is a spot in everyone's mind that should agree. Where everyone ought to agree is that a thorough investigation is needed to ensure public faith in the integrity of future elections. Anybody who observed the fraud as publicized on TV should be concerned.

To that end, renowned economist and White House trade adviser Peter Navarro conducted a forensic analysis of reported election irregularities and he condensed his findings into a 35-page report. I published his offerings with his permission in a book I wrote about a month ago entitled *Stolen Election*.

Yes, Dr. Peter Navarro gave me permission to print his two reports in the book proving without a doubt that Trump was the victor and that the president was scammed by Democrat operatives in the battleground states. Feel free to enjoy this book along with the Kindle copy at https://www.amazon.com/gp/product/B08T49M456

Be advised please that no distilled or condensed report on the election steal is easy to write. I learned that in this exercise. Nonetheless, Mr. Navarro proceeded to collate allegations in battleground states — ranging from outright voter fraud and ballot mishandling to statistical anomalies and dumb mistakes. His points are contained in 50 lawsuits and judicial rulings, thousands of affidavits and declarations, and testimony from various battleground state hearings.

The SCOTUS was well aware and also well aware that Trump had been taken by those who had been trying to impeach him since he walked down the elevators when he announced. If they knew this, they knew enough to accept the case and decide on the side of truth but they did neither.

Peter Navarro does not mince words in his two reports. He concludes that "patterns of election irregularities are so consistent across the six battleground states that they suggest a coordinated strategy to, if not steal the election, strategically game the election process in such a way as to . . . unfairly tilt the playing field in favor of the Biden-Harris ticket." For Americans of both major parties, that is not good news.

Thank you to Dr. Peter Navarro for permission to include parts of his document in this book. navarroreport@protonmail.com

Executive Summary

The Navarro report assesses the fairness and integrity of the 2020 Presidential Election by examining six dimensions of alleged election irregularities across six key battleground states. Evidence used to conduct this assessment includes more than 50 lawsuits and judicial rulings, thousands of affidavits and declarations; as well as testimony in a variety of state venues, published analyses by think tanks and legal centers, videos and photos, public comments, and extensive press coverage. And ask the SCOTUS, in such an important case, how much work did they do?

Navarro created a matrix shown below that indicates that significant irregularities occurred across all six battleground states and across all six dimensions of election irregularities. This finding lends credence to the claim that the election may well have been stolen from President Donald J. Trump.

Brian W. Kelly the author of this book says you can take the words *may well have* out of the above and replace it with was definitely stolen from President Trump and the authorities whose mission it was to determine fraud, simply decided to accede to the demands of the Democrats. Shame ! Shame !

	ARIZONA	GEORGIA	MICHIGAN	NEVADA	PENNSYLVANIA	WISCONSIN
Outright Voter Fraud	✓	✓	*	✓	*	✓
Ballot Mishandling		✓	✓	✓	✓	✓
Contestable Process Fouls	✓	✓	✓	✓	✓	✓
Equal Protection Clause Violations	✓	✓	✓	✓	✓	✓
Voting Machine Irregularities	✓	✓	✓	✓	✓	*
Significant Statistical Anomalies	✓	✓	✓	✓		✓

✓ = Wide-Spread Evidence   * = Some Evidence

From the findings of this report, it is possible to infer what may well have been a coordinated strategy to effectively stack the election deck against the Trump-Pence ticket. Indeed, the observed patterns of election irregularities are so consistent across the six battleground states that they suggest a coordinated strategy to, if not steal the election outright, strategically game the election process in such a way as to "stuff the ballot box" and unfairly tilt the playing field in favor of the Biden-Harris ticket.

Have you heard any of that on a pro-Dem TV station such as MSNBC. Of course not. They were in on the fix.

Was SCOTUS in on the fix? Ask them, please!

Topline findings of this report include:

The weight of evidence and patterns of irregularities are such that it is irresponsible for anyone – especially the mainstream media – to claim there is "no evidence" of fraud or irregularities.

The ballots in question because of the identified election irregularities are more than sufficient to swing the outcome in favor of President Trump should even a relatively small portion of these ballots be ruled illegal.

All six battleground states exhibit most, or all, six dimensions of election irregularities. However, each state has a unique mix of issues that might be considered "most important." To put this another way, all battleground states are characterized by the same or similar election irregularities; but, like Tolstoy's unhappy families, each battleground state is different in its own election irregularity way.

This was theft by a thousand cuts across six dimensions and six battleground states rather than any one single "silver bullet" election irregularity.

In refusing to investigate a growing number of legitimate grievances, the anti-Trump media and censoring social media are complicit in shielding the American public from the truth. This is a dangerous game that simultaneously undermines the credibility of the media and the stability of our political system and Republic.

Those journalists, pundits, and political leaders now participating in what has become a Biden Whitewash should acknowledge the six dimensions of election irregularities and conduct the appropriate investigations to determine the truth about the 2020 election. If this is not done before Inauguration Day, we risk putting into power an illegitimate and illegal president lacking the support of a large segment of the American people.

The failure to aggressively and fully investigate the six dimensions of election irregularities assessed in this report is a signal failure not just of our anti-Trump mainstream media and censoring social media but also of both our legislative and judicial branches.

Republican governors in Arizona and Georgia together with Republican majorities in both chambers of the State Legislatures of five of the six battleground states–Arizona, Georgia, Michigan, Pennsylvania, and Wisconsin – have had both the power and the opportunity to investigate the six dimensions of election irregularities presented in this report. Yet, wilting under intense political pressure, these politicians have failed in their Constitutional duties and responsibilities to do so–and thereby failed both their states and this nation as well as their party.

Both State courts and Federal courts, including the Supreme Court, have failed the American people in refusing to appropriately adjudicate the election irregularities that have come before them. Their failures pose a great risk to the American Republic.

If these election irregularities are not fully investigated prior to Inauguration Day and thereby effectively allowed to stand, this nation runs the very real risk of never being able to have a fair presidential election again – with the down-ballot Senate races scheduled for January 5 in Georgia an initial test case of this looming risk. Post note: The Republicans lost Georgia Senate on January 5, as many believe because the same shenanigans were executed by the Democrats to assure a win.

Concluding Observations

From the findings of this report, it is possible to infer what may well have been a coordinated strategy to effectively stack the election deck against the Trump-Pence ticket. Indeed, the patterns of election irregularities observed in this report are so consistent across the six battleground states that they suggest a coordinated strategy to, if not steal the election, then to strategically game the election process in such a way as to unfairly tilt the playing field in favor of the Biden-Harris ticket.

A major part of this "stuff the ballot box" strategy has been aptly summarized in a complaint filed before the US Supreme Court by the State of Texas: Using the COVID-19 pandemic as a justification, [Democrat] government officials [in Georgia, Michigan, Pennsylvania, and Wisconsin] usurped their legislatures' authority and unconstitutionally revised their state's election statutes.

They accomplished these statutory revisions through executive fiat or friendly lawsuits, thereby weakening ballot integrity. According to the Texas complaint – which the Supreme Court sadly refused to hear–the goal of this strategy was to flood the battleground states "with millions of ballots to be sent through the mails, or placed in drop boxes, with little or no chain of custody." At the same time, Democrat government officials also sought to "weaken the strongest security measures protecting the integrity of the vote signature verification and witness requirements."

The findings of the assessment conducted in the Navarro Immaculate Deception report are consistent with the Texas complaint. Key takeaways include:

The weight of evidence and patterns of irregularities uncovered in this report are such that it is irresponsible for anyone – especially the mainstream media – to claim that there is "no evidence" of fraud or irregularities.

The ballots that have come into question because of the identified election irregularities are more than sufficient to swing the outcome in favor of President Trump should even a relatively small portion of these ballots be ruled illegal.

While all six battleground states exhibit most, or all, six dimensions of election irregularities, each state has a unique mix of issues that might be considered "most important." To put this another way, all battleground states are characterized by the same or similar election irregularities; but, like Tolstoy's unhappy families, each battleground state is different in its own election irregularity way.

This was theft by a thousand cuts across six dimensions and six battleground states rather than any one single "silver bullet" election irregularity.

In refusing to investigate a growing number of legitimate grievances, the anti-Trump media and censoring social media are complicit in shielding the American public from the truth. This is a dangerous game that simultaneously undermines the credibility of the media and the stability of our political system and Republic.

Those journalists, pundits, and political leaders now participating in what has become a Biden Whitewash should acknowledge the election irregularities and conduct the appropriate investigations to determine the truth about the 2020 election. This must be determined before the next election. Already we have put power into an illegitimate and illegal president lacking the support of a large segment of the American people. We have to figure out how to amass the collection of evidence to force officials into never permitting such election rules again.

The failure to aggressively and fully investigate the election irregularities assessed in the Navarro report is a signal failure not just of our anti-Trump mainstream media and censoring social media but also of both our legislative and judicial branches—especially the Supreme Court which could have made it all better simply by hearing the facts.

By now with Biden already in office. We know that Republican governors in Arizona and Georgia together with Republican majorities in both chambers of the State Legislatures of five of the six battleground states–Arizona, Georgia, Michigan, Pennsylvania, and Wisconsin–have had both the power and the opportunity to investigate the irregularities as presented by Peter Navarro.

Yet, there is such persistence by the Democrats and the corrupt media and the corporate titans to silence the forces of truth with intense political pressure, these politicians and jurists have failed in their Constitutional duties and responsibilities to do so–and thereby failed both their states and this nation as well as their party.

Both State courts and Federal courts, including the Supreme Court, have failed the American people in refusing to appropriately adjudicate the election irregularities that have come before them. Their failures pose a great risk to the American Republic. Now that before the end of the first week in office the new President has reversed many of President Trump's very popular accomplishments with his nineteen Executive orders, it is not just speculation that the new administration looks to make this a socialist country. It is now a work in process.

These election irregularities were fully investigated prior to Inauguration Day but the events preceding the inauguration such as the storming of the capital and President Pence's reluctance to act, and the SCOTUS's cowardly retreat have made it substantially more difficult to reverse the problems caused by the election steal. It is already stolen. Nonetheless it cannot be allowed to stand. Without a resolution by fair people, this nation runs the very real risk of never being able to have a fair presidential election again. Even the down-ballot Senate races held on January 5 in Georgia were part of the election theft and it proved how serious resolving this issue will be. Yet, we cannot give up. We must eliminate the Supreme Court and put our best approach forward to gain back control of the US government as we may suffer even more from this looming risk.

Additional Information on the Deception

Here is some additional information. The president is quite disappointed in SCOTUS. In early January he said that the election challenge is not over. The storming of the Capital by Antifa and BLM and other thugs has seemingly put an end to the Trump challenges though they are very valid. It proves that Joe Biden is not our president but Congress says he is.

The major author of the report just presented, White House trade adviser Peter Navarro updated his report about alleged voting irregularities in the 2020 election to include data about Michigan.

The director of the Office of Trade and Manufacturing Policy posted a video on Vimeo recently explaining what he found in the

Wolverine State using additional data and documents that he argues could flip the election from victory for President-elect Joe Biden to another term for President Trump.

"I've concluded that the number of possible illegal votes in the state of Michigan tops 379,000 ballots, more than twice the alleged victory margin of Joe Biden," Navarro said. Biden won the state of Michigan and its 16 Electoral College votes by roughly 150,000 ballots.

The Michigan number mentioned in the video was a missing figure in the original, 36-page report shown above, that Navarro had previously released. Navarro developed his report in his private capacity. As you now know, his investigation found at least 100,000 votes in Arizona, Georgia, Nevada, Pennsylvania, and Wisconsin that could be illegal ballots that, if tossed out, would put Trump over Biden's "victory" margin.

Navarro cited Richard Baris, director of Big Data Poll, who he said found roughly 9,500 Michigan voters "confirmed" to be dead through the Social Security Death Index and about 2,000 voters listed as 100 years old or more who were not listed as "living centenarians" in the state.

Pointing to data from Wayne County, the state's most populous county, Navarro said 174,384 absentee ballots were cast in Detroit with no individual voter registration numbers. Therefore, he said, they were "illegally counted."

Navarro also claimed there were "statistical anomalies," claiming that Trump held a "seemingly insurmountable lead" at midnight on Election Day, followed by "an inexplicable vote surge" of almost 200,000 ballots for Biden, compared to only about 10,000 for Trump.

The findings clash with statements by state and local officials, as well as experts, who have said the ballot counting was transparent and accurate and attributed some allegations of irregularities to clerical errors and not voter fraud. The state of Michigan has committed to an audit of the election. Already a hand audit in Antrim County, where concerns were raised about voting machines, affirmed Trump's victory in that county and netted him an additional 12 votes.

Navarro's investigation is just one facet of a larger operation to question and challenge the results of the election as Trump, his legal team, and Republican allies seek to overturn the results over claims of widespread voter fraud and irregularities, which have not had much success in court.

On a recent Monday, GOP lawmakers huddled with Trump and Vice President Mike Pence at the White House about a long-shot strategy to challenge Biden's win in Congress.

To conclude his roughly two-minute video, Navarro said it is "absolutely critical" for there to be an investigation of the six dimensions of voting irregularities mentioned in the original report, which include: outright voter fraud, ballot mishandling, contestable process fouls, equal protection clause violations, voting machine irregularities, and significant statistical anomalies.

He said some or all of these issues were found in six battleground states and "may well be the greatest political scandal in U.S. presidential history."

ENDNOTES

There is much reference material (ibid; op. cit. stuff, witnesses) for this Immaculate Deception document written mostly by Peter Navarro is viewable at the following reference link. You will also be taken to the original document.

r o

https://bannonswarroom.com/wp-content/uploads/2020/12/The-Immaculate-Deception-12.15.20-1.pdf

Our thank you to Dr. Navarro for permission to reprint parts of this report.

Chapter 9 Peter Navarro Intro to The Art of the Steal

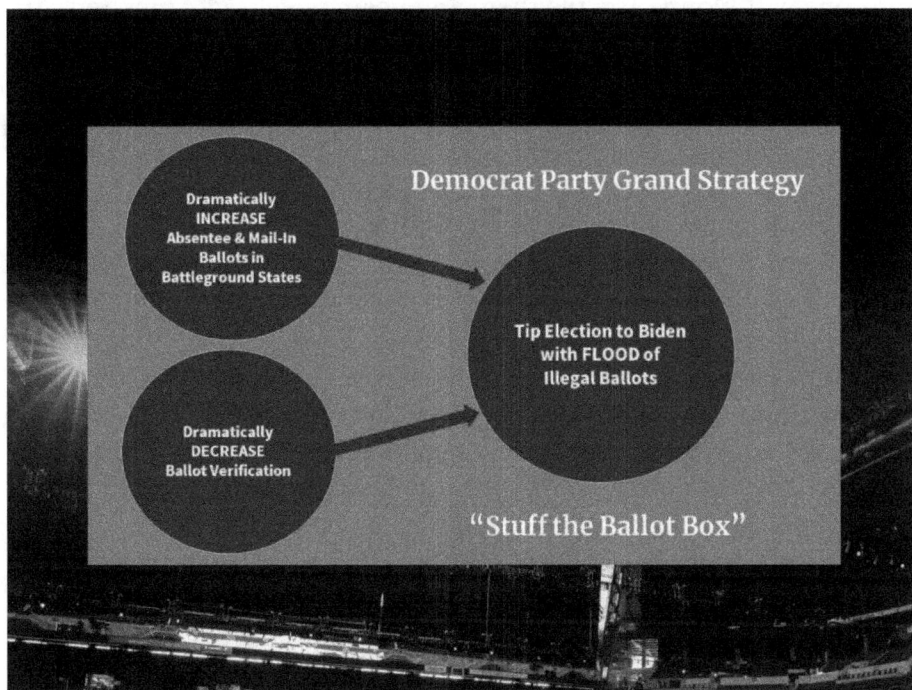

'On January 4, Peter Navarro released his 'Volume Two' of the report on voter fraud allegations. He called this one "The Art of the Steal."

Thank you to Mr. Navarro for permission to reprint parts of this great report in this book

The report had been becoming less and less popular as the mainstream media had been declaring Biden the president

White House trade adviser Peter Navarro was not happy that he had covered all the bases in his groundbreaking report titled "The Immaculate Deception. He released his update, "The Art of the Steal on January 5, only days before the wimpy Republicans gave up on Trump.

By the way, conservatives no longer brag about watching Fox News. We let Donna Brazile speak for the Democrats and have no need to hear her or any of the Fox line of anti-Trump rhetoric. This morning on January 9, NewsMax featured two commentators who definitely said that there was no steal. If NewsMax keeps up with that, I know I for one will Donna Brazile them and begin watching AON and reruns of Gilligan's island rather than NewsMax. Conservatives must stand up for what we believe. .

Navarro released another report on Tuesday January 5 documenting what he considers evidence of the Democratic Party's years long effort to "steal" the 2016 election from President Trump, following up on his December report detailing a ton of illegal votes in the 2020 foray.

Navarro used his sequel report to describe an approach taken by Democrats to increase Joe Biden's "narrow and illegitimate 'victory'" by more than 7 million votes in the general election. It was this plus the Republican Wimps in Congress, which gave Biden 306 Electoral College votes for the record but not for reality.

We know Trump won in his "landslide" 2020 win.

Navarro's report, "The Art of the Steal", was released one day before all hell broke loose at the Capitol. Congress was supposed to meet with supposedly gutsy Republicans. The brave of heart were to object to the fraudulent electors in the battleground states. They promised conservative Americans – the 74,000,000 plus (perhaps 90 million) who voted for Trump that they would do so.

Yes, Republicans in both the House and Senate had promised the people a hearing on the facts even though there were long-odds at overturning the election. They *promised* to give it a shot and to give the world an opportunity to hear their objections based on fact and affidavits.

But, they found the first excuse and just like SCOTUS, most of them chickened out.

The Democratic Party literally stuffed the ballot box as a strategy according to Navarro. The crooks relied on expanding voter access to absentee and mail-in ballots and they unconstitutionally relaxed ballot verification protocols and other impediments to registering to vote.

By the way, Peter Navarro is a great and loyal patriot. He has been a vocal critic of the Wimpy, Gutless, Turncoat Republicans who stopped quivering long enough to criticize Trump over the Democrat planned Capitol storming. Navarro told the Republican Wimps point blank: 'You need to shut up!'

"It is important to point out here that much of what the Democrats did was legal; but some of what they did at times also bent, and arguably sometimes broke, the rules or the law," Navarro wrote as he examined closely the changes they made illegally in Pennsylvania voting laws.

Their effort without the endorsement of the state legislature, expanded access to absentee ballots part of which had been passed by the state's Republican legislature in 2019 and a federal court ruling from 2018 that prevented Georgia from implementing an "exact match" voting law to complete his narrative of an election that was stolen from Trump. The expansion of the laws by non-state legislators is the essence of the unconstitutional acts by the states. What they did was against the law—period.

SCOTUS knew well and understood their acts were unconstitutional. What is SCOTUS' job other than to support the Constitution? That is why I wrote this book. We do not need a SCOTUS with members that will abdicate their duties under the Constitution.

"The practical result of the Democrat Party's two-pronged Grand 'Stuff the Ballot Box' Strategy was to flood the six key battleground states with enough illegal absentee and mail-in ballots to turn a decisive Trump victory into a small alleged Biden 'victory,'" Navarro wrote, referring to Arizona, Georgia, Michigan, Nevada, Pennsylvania, and Wisconsin.

Much of Navarro's fire was targeted on "the corrosive effects" of "Wall Street oligarch George Soros" and the "CCP virus pandemic," but he saved some volleys for "unwitting 'useful idiots'" He was talking about Republicans such as Georgia Secretary of State Brad Raffensperger and Gov. Brian Kemp, whom Navarro claimed "ran the table on behalf of the Democrats."

These useful idiots scammed the Republicans as both officials repeatedly articulated their support for Republican candidates in the Jan. 5 Senate runoff elections. Lies, lies, and more lies. We now know that this too was wrought with fraud. Ask the wimps Loeffler and Perdue. He did not call SCOTUS useful idiots though they certainly served the Democrats in their steal. One day we will coin a phrase to describe what the SCOTUS did. Right now I am happy with the notion of SCOTUS Eliminatus!,

Throughout this great report, Navarro also deviated from his original electoral grudge to criticize federal institutions for failing to attack Trump's political enemies. After all, the election was stolen. There is no doubt about that

"It is as remarkable as it is abhorrent that the Trump Administration's Department of Justice did not conduct a full investigation and issue indictments in a Russia Hoax that ended in a complete exoneration of President Trump," Navarro decried, despite investigations conducted by DOJ Inspector General Michael Horowitz and U.S. Attorney John Durham, who was recently appointed special counsel to investigate "any violations of law related to the inquiries conducted by the FBI's Crossfire Hurricane operation and, later, special counsel Robert Mueller." It was all a corrupt scheme to take down President Trump.

"Volumes 1 and 2 of the Navarro Report — The Immaculate Deception and The Art of the Steal — together make the strong case for a full investigation of the election irregularities and strategic gaming of our political process that have led to the recent a stolen presidential election," Navarro concluded. "

Any such investigation must begin immediately as this nation simply cannot risk the long-term perception that the inauguration of the president was legitimate for it was not. It is already perceived by a large segment of the American people as illegitimate."

SCOTUS had a chance to make it all right but they gave up when John Roberts said the going had gotten too tough to do the right thing.

It may be too late for Trump in 2021 because the Republican turncoats missed their opportunity on January 6. But it is not too late to put the cowards who pulled this off in jail. Now the people are waiting for the next primary so that we can replace all those who did not stand up for Americans with representatives who will be patriots not elitist members of the SWAMP. A lot of Republicans will have their last days in Congress after the next election. Bye Bye Wimps. Before that we can execute SCOTUS Eliminatus.

BTW folks, Trump and Pence had not spoken for about a week since the Wednesday, when Pence stabbed Trump in the back. They are now talking again. At the time, the vice president sheltered in place at the Capitol after the building was stormed by Antifa and BLM and a small number of misguided Trump supporters.

Senator James Inhofe of Oklahoma told the Tulsa World newspaper he'd "never seen Pence as angry" as he was after being blasted by Trump for not intervening in the congressional count of Electoral College votes. Trump tweeted that Pence lacked "courage." Trump is right as usual, Pence pulled off a Republican Wimp stunt. He has no right to be angry but America has a lot to be angry with him about.

Donald Trump, when President was very aware that the media and Big Tech had a major effect on liberal opinions and he was aware that the Democrats said jump and the media and Big Tech consistently shouted loud: "how high?"

He was concerned about having just eight justices and so at least one time this time he explained the need to swiftly replace the late Supreme Court Justice Ruth Bader Ginsburg with Amy Coney Barrett. President Trump was aware that just like the fake news a number of his allies were fake allies. These faux allies resented that they were not invited to the great cocktail parties held by Democrat loyalists. In essence, he could not be sure of a lot of his allies—far too many for him to get a fair shot in his own White House.

Donald Trump said the Court likely would more than likely have to rule on disputes about the presidential election but even he could never have imagined the extent of the election dishonesty played against him. Nonetheless he said: "I think this will end up in the Supreme Court," he told reporters on September 23. "And I think it's very important that we have nine justices....This scam that the Democrats are pulling...will be before the United States Supreme Court.

And I think having a 4–4 situation is not a good situation, if you get that. I don't know that you'd get that. [In other words Trump knew that he might have a few fake allies on the court.] I think it should be 8–nothing or 9–nothing. But just in case it would be more political than it should be, I think it's very important to have a ninth justice."

In Trump's view, a ruling against his campaign would be "more political than it should be," while a ruling in which Barrett voted the way the president who picked her wanted her to vote would be untainted by politics. Trump was no dummy and had grave concerns after Barrett's confirmation, when he cautioned the justices that siding with Biden in a post-election case would threaten their status and power.

"If Sleepy Joe Biden is actually elected President," he tweeted, "the 4 Justices (plus1) that helped make such a ridiculous win possible would be relegated to sitting on not only a heavily PACKED COURT, but probably a REVOLVING COURT as well."

Trump did believe that Barrett should dance with the one that brought her. But in case that argument was not persuasive enough, he argued that it was in her personal and professional interest to prevent Biden from taking office. In the end, however, Barrett joined the rest of the Court, including Trump's two other nominees and three justices appointed by Republicans George H.W. Bush and George W. Bush, in declining to hear two cases that sought to overturn Biden's victory.

That folks is why I wrote this book. Barrett and the rest should be embarrassed for being the scared wimps that they are and before the SCOTUS Eliminatus plan, they should resign to appease the negative feelings of the people whose trust they need.

Trump who had always been confident when he saw the extent of the steal knew he would win in court if given a fair hearing. SCOTUS made sure he got no hearing. The President seemed genuinely dismayed by those outcomes. "The fact that the Supreme Court wouldn't find standing in an original jurisdiction matter between multiple states, and including the President of the States, is absurd," he tweeted after the justices turned away Texas Attorney General Ken Paxton's challenge to the election results in four swing states.

"They just 'chickened out' and didn't want to rule on the merits of the case. So bad for our Country!"

Amen, President Trump. You got it right!

Trump later upped the ante in his opinion of the SCOTUS, saying the justices—including the three that he appointed—are "totally incompetent and weak" as well as chicken-hearted. "We have absolute PROOF" of "massive Election Fraud," he said, "but they don't want to see it…No 'standing,' they say. If we have corrupt elections, we have no country!"

Trump's complaint that the justices won't even consider his "absolute PROOF" implies that they would have been compelled to side with him if only they had taken up Paxton's case and/or the lawsuit in which Rep. Mike Kelly (R–Pa.) sought to overturn Pennsylvania's election results.

Some ask this—if the justices (again, including the ones Trump himself picked) are as cowardly, weak, and incompetent as Trump portrays them, what would have stopped them from rejecting these lawsuits on the merits if they had heard the case? I'll tell you what—they would have been forced to see the dirty hands of the Democrats running all over their well-orchestrated election fraud. If they ruled against the truth, the people would know and it would be worse than not accepting the case on mystery grounds amounting too "we're too weak and scared."

Given the reality of what occurred and the preponderance of evidence favoring the fact that there was immense fraud involved, one can say that again Trump's arguments are compelling. He did not just argue that the 2020 presidential election was perverted by massive fraud; he also suggested that the judicial system is partisan and corrupt enough to not accept tough evidence, rejecting compelling arguments because they were difficult to hear and follow, not because they lacked merit.

Trump is right and I heard much of the proof in many of the often televised hearings. Some hearings I viewed multiple times. Did SCOTUS do as much? Anybody who took the time, including jurists, would have come to the correct conclusions also—unless of course—they feared ANTIFA and BLM and other potential rioters.

"It is historically, mathematically, politically, and logically impossible" that Biden won the election, Trump insisted in a video he posted on Facebook. Check it out and you can't help agreeing.

"We won this election by a magnificent landslide, and the people of the United States know it." He said he was "determined to pursue every legal and constitutional option available to stop the theft of the presidential election." God help us if a fair hearing of the evidence even in a civilian court cannot definitely show the fraud. Books like this and others will help but we need a commission appointed to run down all of the irregularities so there is no doubt in anybody's mind.

Many of the remedies were exhausted by the inertia of the courts. By the time the Georgia steal came about, there were not many Trump options left. Of course it would have been helpful to be able to have a Justice Department investigation of the voting machines, with perhaps attorney Sidney Powell, and Lin Wood who are both known for winning long-shots, to investigate additional charges of election fraud.

Pence of course could have sent electors back to the states, by January 5 but he did not. So, the only real big play remaining for Trump was to challenge the electoral votes when they were brought to be tallied by Congress on January 6.

However, as we know the friends of the Democrats such as ANTIFA and BLM, colluded to make January 6 a circus by storming the US Capitol. This aided wimpish Republican RINOS to conveniently forget their promise to the people to reject electors who were illegitimate.

Democrats out-chicanered the honest efforts of brave Republicans again and made the rest of the Republicans feel small if they chose not to damn Trump along with leader McConnell, Nancy Pelosi, Chuck Schumer and the Dems for "inciting a riot." Hard to believe that Republicans fell for the ploy. Grown men duped by the Democrats who had nothing to gain but power. Duped again. The Dems know how to win by hook or by crook—either!

Pundits who hate Trump will see it differently as they did for the past five years of the Russian, Ukrainian, and Chinese hoaxes that were bought by so many it is hard to believe those convinced were over the age of reason. These people would say that Trump had a fair hearing and he exhausted every legal and constitutional option. And the moon has a never ending supply of green cheese.

They would say the President is not going to suddenly admit that he lost the election. Of course not, it was stolen from him by Democrats. They hate Trump so much the best they can say is that Trump, after losing would "continue to loudly decry an electoral system that was blatantly rigged against him, a judicial branch that could not be trusted to reveal the truth, and of course Justice Department officials who were shockingly incurious about the greatest crime in U.S. history.

Trump would also have harsh words for journalists who were blinded by their hatred of him and Republican politicians who prematurely threw in the towel after promising the people they would reject electors in the battleground states. He would have lots of reasons for being unhappy and expressing it. So do I. And so do most of those reading this book and my hit book *Stolen Election*.

Before you believe any of that crap folks, remember that the people in the media have been producing fake news for five years now. This would just be a continuation. Tell me you do not—all of a sudden— trust the media and the Never Trumpers? I think not. Why do all your neighbors have a lump in their throat now after just nineteen executive orders?

Has anybody seen president Biden around recently.

Chapter 10 Implementing SCOTUS Eliminatus

Citizens from time to time have been uninspired by the Supreme Court's nondescript and anti-people rulings such as recently in its rulings against hearing cases connected to the biggest election scandal in US history. The cases were filed on behalf of the Donald Trump Legal team. Uninspired to say the least, many regular Joes have been grumbling privately and publicly about how the court could turn its back on over 75 million voters by not hearing the Texas v Battleground States case.

This of course brought forth the question: How can we get rid of the Supreme Court since it has failed to do the job for which we pay it? This then led to the question: "Can a Supreme Court justice be removed? In fact, Can the whole court be removed?

The answer is yes, the court can be removed by removing one justice at a time for cause. This process is similar to how the impeachment of all other government officials would take place, including the president. It is still known as impeachment. Impeachment is rare but possible for SC justices. I have some other ideas.

Those who watched the confirmation hearings of U.S. Supreme Court nominee Brett Kavanaugh and, and Amy Cony Barrett, for no particular reason, were wondering if it was possible to remove a Supreme Court justice after he or she was confirmed to his lifetime appointment. The answer again is yes. The framers of the U.S. Constitution included a process to do just that. That said, it has never really been done successfully. But, it can be done.

Check out Section 1 of Article 3 of the Constitution. It says "The judicial Power of the United States, shall be vested in one supreme Court, and in such inferior Courts as the Congress may from time to time ordain and establish. The Judges, both of the supreme and inferior Courts, shall hold their offices during good behavior, and shall, at stated times, receive for their services a compensation which shall not be diminished during their continuance in office.

This means that the justices hold office as long as they choose and can only be removed from office by impeachment. The only Justice to be impeached was back in 1805, when Associate Justice Samuel Chase–who was appointed by President George Washington–was accused of allowing his political views to interfere with his decisions and "tending to prostitute" the court and his position. Anybody very curious of the Chase case can read the riveting account on the U.S. Senate's website.

The House of Representatives passed Articles of Impeachment against him, but he was acquitted by the Senate. Not guilty! This is similar to what happened to President Trump about a year ago and to President Clinton just over twenty-years ago. Since we understand what happened to Trump because it is so close-to the present and the silly Dems in Congress are at it again, let's examine the Clinton impeachment briefly.

http://academic.brooklyn.cuny.edu/history/johnson/clintontimelin e.htm

The Clinton timeline for those interested is in the above link

Overall after coming on as an unpaid intern in June 1995, Monica Lewinsky soon met President Clinton and commenced an affair with the former president while he was president. It began in November, 1995. In summer 1996, Linda Tripp was made aware of the Clinton affair by Ms. Lewinsky. The tryst allegedly continued until December 28, 1997, when Lewinsky made her final visit to the White House, according to White House sign-in logs.

For this visit, she was signed in by Ms. Betty Currie. Clinton's secretary and reportedly admitted to Linda Tripp that she had met privately with Clinton who allegedly encouraged her to be "evasive" in her answers in the Jones' lawsuit which was brewing at the time. Lewinsky and her family were ultimately offered immunity for testimony in the Paula Jones Case which most of the public has conveniently forgotten.

Tripp and Lewinsky met often to discuss aspects of the Clinton affair. Tripp recorded the conversations. Ken Starr was the lead investigator. His work ultimately led to the impeachment of President Clinton. Despite his impeachment by the House, the president was acquitted in the subsequent trial before the United States Senate as all 45 Democrats and 10 Republicans voted to acquit.

The prosecution just like today, needed a two-thirds majority to convict but failed to achieve even a bare majority. Rejecting the first charge of perjury, 45 Democrats and 10 Republicans voted "not guilty," and on the charge of obstruction of justice the Senate was split 50-50. After the trial concluded, President Clinton said he was "profoundly sorry" for the burden his behavior imposed on Congress and the American people.

President Trump impeached December 18, 2019

President Trump was impeached by the House on bogus charges about a "perfect" phone call to the Ukraine. There was no reasoning with hateful Democrats. After weeks of discussions among legislators, the House of Representatives voted to impeach the 45th President, Donald Trump, for alleged abuse of power and obstruction of Congress. The vote fell largely along party lines in the House: 230

in favor, 197 against and 1 present. Trump became only the third president ever to be impeached, joining Andrew Johnson and Bill Clinton.

While the country was beginning its battle with COVID-19, the Democrats continued their obsessive lunacy and finally brought the articles of impeachment to the US Senate. Congress did not act in any way to understand or help with the COVID-19 trauma as its obsession with getting rid of Trump was all-consuming. They forgot why they were elected. Just a reminder it was to do the official business of the people.

On February 5, 2020 Trump was acquitted by a trial in the US Senate. Many of us watched the Schiff charade. . The vote was the final step in a two-week ordeal marked by impassioned arguments from House Democrats that President Trump was a danger to the nation. Stalwart support was all that came from Senate Republicans with great presentations by the Legal Team.

RINO Mitt Romney, who needs a psyche examination, IMHO, took sides with the Democrats shaming all Republicans. On February 5, it was all over until this year, two weeks before Trump's term was over. The crazy Democrats in the House decided to impeach Donald Trump again even though his term was up and there was no evidence presented. The Senate had announced that it would not convene to conduct a trial, which is necessary for impeachment.

It was not until after the Biden Inauguration that the Senate could convene to hear the matter presented by the house. The problem is that Trump will be citizen Trump at the time and all times hence unless reelected, and the Constitution has no rules for impeaching private citizens. I have a couple old girlfriends who I think should be impeached. But, we won't go there.

The House on January 25, brought the impeachment charges to the Senate at 6:55 p.m. ET for a trial which seems less likely to happen as time goes by. Trump is no longer in office. Mitt Romney of course hates Trump and is a deranged person with so much Trump-hate that he backs the charges. Romney's career is over. What conservative needs him.

Meanwhile a growing number of Republican Senators say they are opposed to the proceeding. It looks like the former president will not be convicted on the charge that he incited a siege of the U.S. Capitol. A review of the facts by anybody proves the riot began long before Trump's speech was finished and before he suggested they go to the Capitol.

Democrats are still hoping that the unfounded strong Republican denunciations of Trump after the Jan. 6 riot will translate into a conviction and a separate vote to bar Trump from holding office again. Nobody with a sound mind expects Trump to be impeached especially because the Constitution's prescribed punishment would be removal from office and Trump is already gone.

The Washington Examiner offered these thoughts:

> Democrats claim to want to unify the country, but impeaching a former president, a private citizen, is the antithesis of unity. This impeachment is nothing more than a partisan exercise designed to divide the country further.
>
> They have brazenly appointed an openly pro-impeachment Democrat to preside over the trial. This is not fair or impartial, and it hardly encourages any kind of unity for the country.
>
> If we are about to try to impeach a president, then where is the chief justice? If the accused is no longer president, then where is the constitutional power to impeach him?
>
> Private citizens don't get impeached. Impeachment is for removal from office, and the accused here has already left office.

My reason for discussing impeachment in this chapter is because it is one of the prescribed ways to remove a SCOTUS Justice. Let me refresh in your minds the utmost dereliction of duty provided by the SCOTUS in not taking the case to resolve the greatest scandal in the history of elections in our country. The SCOTUS needs to be ashamed of itself. After the recitation of the decision not to decide, I will offer my additional thoughts on how the people can best rid ourselves of a Supreme Court that is too afraid to do its job.

Supreme Court Decides Not to Decide

The Supreme Court on Monday December 11 rejected efforts by President Donald Trump and his allies to get the court to quickly consider challenges to President-elect Joe Biden's victory in the November election, effectively shutting the door on the president's last-ditch legal strategy to overturn his defeat. It is a shame.

Justice Thomas and Justice Alito seem to have agreed agree with the bulk of the citizens of the country. However the pundits say the vote was 9-0. About that I do not understand so I include them in the SCOTUS Eliminatus tally.

Here is the ruling which like December 7, 1941 will go down in infamy:

ORDER IN PENDING CASE 155, ORIG. TEXAS V. PENNSYLVANIA, ET AL. The State of Texas's motion for leave to file a bill of complaint is denied for lack of standing under Article III of the Constitution. Texas has not demonstrated a judicially cognizable interest in the manner in which another State conducts its elections. All other pending motions are dismissed as moot.

Statement of Justice Alito, with whom Justice Thomas joins: In my view, we do not have discretion to deny the filing of a bill of complaint in a case that falls within our original jurisdiction. See Arizona v. California, 589 U. S. ___ (Feb. 24, 2020) (Thomas, J., dissenting). I would therefore grant the motion to file the bill of complaint but would not grant other relief, and I express no view on any other issue.

It similarly denied requests from the conservative counsel. Lin Wood and Sidney Powell to expedite challenges to the elections in Michigan and Georgia, as well as other suits filed by Trump supporters.

People listen to speakers during a Stop the Steal rally in front of the Supreme Court on Tuesday, Jan. 5, 2021 in Washington, DC.
Kent Nishimura | Los Angeles Times | Getty Images

The court forgot is role of being the arbiter of truth and justice in America. It expressed a fear of being attacked by rioters from ANTIFA and BLM if it had ruled favorably on any Trump request.

No citizen in America wants any court to decide anything based on personal intimidation. American Citizens want this Supreme Court abolished and rebuilt with Patriots who stand more on reality than on Supreme Court bull----.

I think you got it Justice Roberts. Don't worry I am not suggesting anybody visit your home with vengeance in their hearts. But, I question why you think you have a right to continue not only as Chief justice but as a member of the most prestigious team of Jurists ever assembled by the patriots—The Supreme Court of the US.

The Beatles once said, "Don't let me down." CJ Roberts, you did worse, you let us all down to serve your own deep personal fears proving that a Milktoast should not serve on the Supreme Court. . I urge you to step down and ask your fellow associate justices to make that big step with you.

That would be the easy way with the least embarrassment.

If you and your associate justices will not step down, which is the recommended approach from the majority of the voters of the US, without having all the answers, I, your humble author will agree to take this case. I will judge you, Dr. Robert, and your court of the prissiest with few words but with the full rationale that can be filled in after the court, the court once led by CJ Roberts the soon to be impeached, is dismissed.

I am not an advocate of SCOTUS impeachment. Let me cover a little Trump ground first. I have a better plan. For instance, in Trump v. Boockvar, one of the cases challenging the Pennsylvania election procedures, the president's attorney, John Eastman, urged the court in a December brief to take up the case before Jan. 6, when Congress met to finalize the Electoral College tally. None of this mattered to this scaredy-cat SCOTUS. Tell me why the people who believe Biden is Bad and Trump is good should feel good about a SCOTUS that seems to love Biden and hate Trump—unfair for sure!

The legal challenges that the Supreme Court refused to expedite included a challenge from Kelli Ward, head of the Arizona Republican Party, to the Electoral Count Act; a challenge from Rep. Mike Kelly, R-Pa., to no-excuse mail-in voting in his state; and two complaints brought by ex-Trump attorney Powell regarding the elections in Michigan and Georgia.

The too-scared SCOTUS – John Roberts & company, shot down great ideas because John Roberts had told the associate justices, which he commanded, that being scared to act was just as good as deciding to act.

Before you are all impeached, why not impeach the CJ yourselves unless you are part of the problem. You already proved you are not part of the solution. That's why the SCOTUS Eliminatus implementation now must be in force.

Sidney Powell had proven that among other things, deceased Venezuelan leader Hugo Chavez was in on a plot to rig the 2020 contest, and she was hit with a $1.3 billion defamation suit by Dominion Voting Systems, a voting machine supplier that many

Trump supporters believe signed the death warrant to Trump's voting lead. Sidney Powell and he co-counsel Lin Wood are great lawyers.

President Trump wanted Atty Powell to be his special counsel to investigate election fraud. CNBC says she does not respond to them. So what! Why should she return pleas from CNBC, a fake news provider, for their requests for comment. They are not for America. They are as we all know, a fake news organization

Wood and Powell got no respect from the popular corrupt media. Just recently both had their Twitter accounts suspended by the Big Tech Corporate Tyrants. Trump had his account suspended so it is an honor for Powell and Wood to also be affected in this social media crackdown on those outlets and legal beagles who are spreading the truth about the election.

The SCOTUS also refused to expedite three cases filed by the Trump campaign -- two challenges to mail-in ballot rules in Wisconsin and one challenge to eased voting rules in Pennsylvania. Those suits properly argued that the changed rules in PA were not made by the legislature. They also increased the likelihood of voter fraud. There was more fraud than ever in this past election. SCOTUS knew and well understood this.

However, because CJ Roberts put the fear of God in them that ANTIFA and BLM would harm them if they did what was right and just, the associate justices hid behind Roberts' robes so they would not be hurt by predators against our nation. Trump had been the only president in years and still is the only one who fights for the good and the safety of all Americans—even SCOTUS justices who rule against him with no reason.

While Trump argued that there was widespread voter fraud in the 2020 election, his deep state Department of Justice, sided with the deep state on the issue and punted like the cowards they are.. They opted to take no action on any of the items of truth discovered

So what do we do with Scotus?

The reality of 2021 and onward to 2022 or perhaps to 2024 is that the Democrats or as some would say, the DEMO**Rats** are in charge of America. On January 25, 2021, the orders against American by Joe Biden, President had already reached 19. There are more coming. We can address an inactive SCOTUS right here and now even if Team Biden will not bring it in. No President can lead the country (USA) without a majority in favor of his or her actions.

So, what do we do with SCOTUS? The current SCOTUS has gotten too comfortable in their ugly skins for the people to stand now that they are pompous keisters aligned with those who no longer care about the regular people in the US. What a shame for sure. Why can't what ought to be, be what it ought to be?

Since I am not a Congressman though I once ran for Congress, I understand that the people own the power. But the people are often not enough to stop injustice. If I had the funding of the people advocates, instead of the funding a of a plebeian of modest means, I would offer the following precepts on how to solve the problem:

Precepts

1. In all cases, the nine current justices would be retired. Ask all members of SCOTUS to resign from office because they did not serve the more than 75,000,000 Americans well. They permitted ANTIFA and BLM and other riot-prone organizations to scare them to act against their best nature and CJ Roberts concurred.

If they will not resign from precept 1, execute precept 2

2. Form a commission from private dollars—admittedly easier said than done—that offers a deal to the Democrats. This is an alternative to stuffing the Court. In essence this would result in the Republicans giving up its 6-3 majority of conservatives and giving the Democrats the John Roberts slot. Democrats would then have four justices and

Republicans would have five. Roberts is really a Democrat anyway. This would formalize the role of his Supreme court slot.

To effect this change, Democrats and Republicans impeach all nine members of the Supreme Court and when the party's pick replacement jurists. Democrats pick four and Republicans pick five. So in essence in order to get unanimous concurrence on unseating the current SCOTUS, Republicans give up one seat and Democrats agree to gain one seat. The new justices would give Republicans a 5-4 advantage. Democrats would get another seat without having to wait until somebody dies and needs to be replaced.

Right now, the SCOTUS is technically in conservative hands (6-3) according to most. But there are a number of Associate Justices who do not act like the people expect. For example John Roberts votes with Democrats making the effective SCOTUS balance 5-4.They would be fired to begin the process.

As noted, Justice John Roberts is not a conservative. The Liberals have just three associate justices right now. How about if the new Supreme Court after we fire all nine justices and they accept it has a 5-4 balance instead of 6-3?

Conservatives would surely agree to give John Robert's current Associate Justice slot to the Democrats because it has falsely been counted as a conservative slot which it is not. .

How does that sound?

Five real conservatives picked by conservatives and four real liberals picked by the liberals.

And the current SCOTUS is in the past.

That means they would never again need to make a decision that would give them agita.

Other Books by Brian W. Kelly (amazon.com, and Kindle)

SCOTUS Interruptus A supreme court cannot refuse to hear critical cases! Eliminate SCOTUS ASAP!
The Corruption in the Wilkes-Barre Area School District--about toxic corruption and stinky things
Stolen Election ??? Democrats say: "fair and just;" Republican cowards surrender to Democrats
The Ten Commandments of Calipered Kinematically Aligned Total Knee Arthroplasty Color Edition
The Ten Commandments of Calipered Kinematically Aligned Total Knee Arthroplasty B/W Edition
About Alexa! Tell me how!
Chronicle of Inept Governance & Corrective Actions from a school board from hell
Hey Alexa! Create me my own personal musical paradise
The Big Toxic School at Little Chernobyl Unpublished with new book (Corruption in WBASD)
FTC Case: LetsGoPublish.com v Amazon Fourth Edition big bully censored nine books
FTC Case: LetsGoPublish.com v Amazon Third Edition big bully censored nine books
FTC Case: LetsGoPublish.com v Amazon Second Edition big bully censored nine books
The President Donald J. Trump Book Catalog   Color Version by Brian Kelly & Lets Go Publish!
The President Donald J. Trump Book Catalog B/W Version by Brian Kelly & Lets Go Publish!
FTC Case: LetsGoPublish.com v Amazon Original case bully censored nine books
What America Wins if Biden Wins Everything!!!!!! The answer is really nothing.
What America Loses if Trump Loses None of the 1000s of Trump wins for starters
**What America Wins When Trump Wins Trump gave the country many benefits and blessings We
Love Trump! Don't you? The President given to the people by God as the answer to our prayers**
Amazon: The Biggest Bully in Town bully blocked eight books in 2020 by most published author
Trump Assured 2020 Victory President needs these two prongs for his platform for landslide
2020 Republican Convention—Speeches Blocked by Amazon Includes memento free Link
2020 RNC Convention Full Speech Transcripts Blocked by Amazon Memento of the 87 best
COVID-19 Mask, Yes? Or No? It's Everybody's Recommended Solution!!!
LSU Tigers Championship Seasons Starts at beginning of LSU Football to the National Championship
Great Coaches in LSU Football Book starts with the first LSU coach; goes to Orgeron Championship
Great Players in LSU Football Begins with 1893 QB Ruffin G Pleasant to 2019 QB Burrow
America for Millennialsl A growing # of disintegrationists want to tear US down
Great Moments in LSU Football Book starts at start of Football to the Ed Orgeron Championship.
The Constitution's Role in a Return to Normalcy Can the Constitution Survive?
The Constitution vs. The Virus Simultaneous attack coronavirus and US governors
One, Two, Three, Pooph!!! Reopen Country Now! Return to normalcy is just around the corner.
Reopen America Now Return to Normalcy
Enough is Enough!Re Re: Covid, We are not children. We're adults.We'll make the right decisions.
How to Write Your 1st Book & Publish it Using Amazon KDP You can do it
REMDESIVIR A Ray of Hope
When Will America Reopen for Business? This author's opinion includes voices of experts
HydroxyChloroquine: The Game Changer
Super Bowl & NFL Championship Seasons The KC Chiefs From the 1st to Super Bowl LIV
Great Coaches in Kansas City Chiefs Football First Coach era to Andy Reid Era
Great Players in Kansas City Chiefs Football From the AFL to Andy Reid Era
Reopen America Now! How to Shut-Down Corona Virus & Return to Normalcy!
Why is Everybody Moving to the Villages? You can afford a home in the Villages
<u>CORONAVIRUS The Cause & the Cure.</u> Many solutions—but which ones will work?
<u>Great Moments in Kansas City Chiefs Football.</u> From the beginning to the Andy Reid Era
How the Philadelphia Eagles Lost Its Karma. This is the one place that tells the story
Cancel All Student Debt Now! Good for America, Good for the Economy.
Social Security Screw Job!!! Scandal: Seniors Intentionally Screwed by US Government
Trump Hate They hate Trump Supporters; Trump; & God—in that order
Christmas Wings for Brian A heartwarming story of a boy whose shoulders kept growing
Merry Christmas to Wilkes-Barre 50 Ways" for Mayor George Brown to Create a Better City.
Air Force Football Championship Seasons From AF Championship to Coach Calhoun's latest team
Syracuse Football Championship Seasons beginning of SU championships; goes to Dino Babers Era
Navy Football Championship Seasons 1st Navy Championships to the Ken Niumatalolo Era
Army Football Championship Seasons Beginning of Football championships to Jeff Monken Era
Florida Gators Championship Seasons Beginning of Football through championships to Dan Mullen era
Alabama's Championship Seasons Beginning of Football past the 2017/2018 National Championship
Clemson Tigers Championship Seasons Beginning of Football to the Clemson National Championships
Penn State's Championship Seasons PSU's first championship to the James Franklin era
Notre Dame's Championship Seasons Before Knute Rockne and past Lou Holtz's 1988 undisputed title
Super Bowls & Championship Seasons: The New York Giants Many championships of the Giants.
Super Bowls & Championship Seasons: New England Patriots Many championships of the Patriots.
Super Bowls & Championship Seasons: The Pittsburgh Steelers Many championship of the Steelers
Super Bowls & Championship Seasons: The Philadelphia Eagles Many championships of the Eagles.

The Big Toxic School Wilkes-Barre Area's Tale of Corruption, Deception, Taxation & Tyranny

Great Players in New York Giants Football Begins with great players of 1925 to the Saquon Barqley era.

Great Coaches in New York Giants Football Begins with Bob Folwell 1925 and to Pat Shurmur in 2019.

Great Moments in New York Giants Football Beginning of Football to the Pat Shurmur era.

Hasta La Vista California Give California its independence.

IT's ALL OVER! Mueller: NO COLLUSION!"—Top Dems going to jail for the hoax!

Democrat Secret for Power & Winning Elections Open borders adds millions of new Democrat Voters

Hope for Wilkes-Barre—John Q. Doe—Next Mayor of Wilkes-Barre

The John Doe Plan & WB Plan will help create a better city!

Great Moments in New England Patriots Football Second Edition

This book begins at the beginning of Football and goes to the Bill Belichick era.

The Cowardly Congress Corrupt US Congress is against America and Americans.

Great Players in Air Force Football From the beginning to the current season

Great Coaches in Air Force Football Grom the beginning to Coach Troy Calhoun

Help for Mayor George and Next Mayor of Wilkes-Barre How to vote for the next Mayor Council

Ghost of Wilkes-Barre Future: Spirit's advice for residents how to pick the next Mayor and Council

Great Players in Air Force Football: Air Force's best players of all time

Great Coaches in Air Force Football: From Coach 1 to Coach Troy Calhoun

Great Moments in Air Force Football: From day 1 to today

Great Players in Navy Football: Navy's best including Bellino & Staubach

Great Coaches in Navy Football: From Coach #39 Ken Niumatalolo

Great Moments in Navy Football: From day 1 to coach Ken Niumatalolo l

No Tree! No Toys! No Toot! Heartwarming story. Christmas gone while 19 month old napped

How to End DACA, Sanctuary Cities, & Resident Illegal Aliens . best solution remove shadowsAmerica.

Government Must Stop Ripping Off Seniors' Social Security!: Hey buddy, seniors can't spare a dime?

Special Report: Solving America's Student Debt Crisis!: The only real solution to the $1.52 Trillion debt

The Winning Political Platform for America Unique winning approach to solve big problems in America.

Lou Barletta v Bob Casey for US Senate Barletta's unique approach to solve big problems in America.

John Chrin v Matt Cartwright for Congress Chrin has a unique approach to solve big problems in America.

The Cure for Hate !!! Can the cure be any worse than this disease that is crippling America?

Andrew Cuomo's Time to Go? He Was Never that Great!": Cuomo says America never that great

White People Are Bad! Bad! Bad! Whoever thought a popular slogan in 2018 *It's OK to be White!*

The Fake News Media Is Also Corrupt !!!: Fake press / media today is not worthy to be 4th Estate.

God Gave US Donald Trump? Trump was sent from God as the people's answer

Millennials Say America Was Never That Great": Too many pleased days of political chumps not over!

It's Time for The John Q. Doe Party… Don't you think? By Elephants.

Great Players in Florida Gators Football… Tim Tebow and a ton of other great players

Great Coaches in Florida Gators Football… The best coaches in Gator history.

The Constitution by Hamilton, Jefferson, Madison, et al. The Real Constitution

The Constitution Companion. Will help you learn and understand the Constitution

Great Coaches in Clemson Football The best Clemson Coaches right to Dabo Swinney

Great Players in Clemson Football The best Clemson players in history

Winning Back America. America's been stolen and can be won back completely

The Founding of America… Great book to pick up a lot of great facts

Defeating America's Career Politicians. The scoundrels need to go.

Midnight Mass by Jack Lammers… You remember what it was like Great story

The Bike by Jack Lammers… Great heartwarming Story by Jack

Wipe Out All Student Loan Debt--Now! Watch the economy go boom!

No Free Lunch Pay Back Welfare! Why not pay it back?

Deport All Millennials Now!!! Why they deserve to be deported and/or saved

DELETE the EPA, Please! The worst decisions to hurt America

Taxation Without Representation 4th Edition Should we throw the TEA overboard again?

Four Great Political Essays by Thomas Dawson

Top Ten Political Books for 2018… Cliffnotes Version of 10 Political Books

Top Six Patriotic Books for 2018… Cliffnotes version of 6 Patriotic Boosk

Why Trump Got Elected!.. It's great to hear about a great milestone in America!

The Day the Free Press Died. Corrupt Press Lives on!

Solved (Immigration) The best solutions for 2018

Solved II (Obamacare, Social Security, Student Debt) Check it out; They're solved.

Great Moments in Pittsburgh Steelers Football... Six Super Bowls and more.

Great Players in Pittsburgh Steelers Football ,,,Chuck Noll, Bill Cowher, Mike Tomin, etc.

Great Coaches in New England Patriots Football,,, Bill Belichick the one and only plus others

Great Players in New England Patriots Football… Tom Brady, Drew Bledsoe et al.

Great Coaches in Philadelphia Eagles Football..Andy Reid, Doug Pederson & Lots more

Great Players in Philadelphia Eagles Football Great players such as Sonny Jurgenson

Great Coaches in Syracuse Football All the greats including Ben Schwartzwalder

Great Players in Syracuse Football. Highlights best players such as Jim Brown & Donovan McNabb

Millennials are People Too !!! Give US millennials help to live American Dream

Brian Kelly for the United States Senate from PA: Fresh Face for US Senate
The Candidate's Bible. Don't pray for your campaign without this bible
Rush Limbaugh's Platform for Americans… Rush will love it
Sean Hannity's Platform for Americans… Sean will love it
Donald Trump's New Platform for Americans. Make Trump unbeatable in 2020
Tariffs Are Good for America! One of the best tools a president can have
Great Coaches in Pittsburgh Steelers Football Sixteen of the best coaches ever to coach in pro football.
Great Moments in New England Patriots Football Great football moments from Boston to New England
Great Moments in Philadelphia Eagles Football. The best from the Eagles from the beginning of football.
Great Moments in Syracuse Football The great moments, coaches & players in Syracuse Football
Boost Social Security Now! Hey Buddy Can You Spare a Dime?
The Birth of American Football. From the first college game in 1869 to the last Super Bowl
Obamacare: A One-Line Repeal Congress must get this done.
A Wilkes-Barre Christmas Story A wonderful town makes Christmas all the better
A Boy, A Bike, A Train, and a Christmas Miracle A Christmas story that will melt your heart
Pay-to-Go   America-First Immigration Fix
Legalizing Illegal Aliens Via Resident Visas Americans-first plan saves $Trillions. Learn how!
60 Million Illegal Aliens in America!!! A simple, America-first solution.
The Bill of Rights By Founder James Madison Refresh *your knowledge of the specific rights for all*
Great Players in Army Football Great Army Football played by great players..
Great Coaches in Army Football Army's coaches are all great.
Great Moments in Army Football Army Football at its best.
Great Moments in Florida Gators Football Gators Football from the start. This is the book.
Great Moments in Clemson Football CU Football at its best. This is the book.
Great Moments in Florida Gators Football Gators Football from the start. This is the book.
The Constitution Companion. A Guide to Reading and Comprehending the Constitution
The Constitution by Hamilton, Jefferson, & Madison – Big type and in English
PATERNO: The Dark Days After Win # 409. Sky began to fall within days of win # 409.
JoePa 409 Victories: Say No More! Winningest Division I-A football coach ever
American College Football: The Beginning From before day one football was played.
Great Coaches in Alabama Football Challenging the coaches of every other program!
Great Coaches in Penn State Football the Best Coaches in PSU's football program
Great Players in Penn State Football The best players in PSU's football program
Great Players in Notre Dame Football The best players in ND's football program
Great Coaches in Notre Dame Football The best coaches in any football program
Great Players in Alabama Football from Quarterbacks to offensive Linemen Greats!
Great Moments in Alabama Football AU Football from the start. This is the book.
Great Moments in Penn State Football PSU Football, start--games, coaches, players,
Great Moments in Notre Dame Football ND Football, start, games, coaches, players
Cross Country with the Parents A great trip from East Coast to West with the kids
Seniors, Social Security & the Minimum Wage. Things seniors need to know.
How to Write Your First Book and Publish It with CreateSpace. You too can be an author.
The US Immigration Fix--It's all in here. Finally, an answer.
I had a Dream IBM Could be #1 Again The title is self-explanatory
WineDiets.Com Presents The Wine Diet Learn how to lose weight while having fun.
Wilkes-Barre, PA; Return to Glory Wilkes-Barre City's return to glory
Geoffrey Parsons' Epoch... The Land of Fair Play Better than the original.
The Bill of Rights 4 Dummmies! This is the best book to learn about your rights.
Sol Bloom's Epoch …Story of the Constitution The best book to learn the Constitution
America 4 Dummmies! All Americans should read to learn about this great country.
The Electoral College 4 Dummmies! How does it really work?
The All-Everything Machine Story about IBM's finest computer server.
ThankYou IBM! This book explains how IBM was beaten in the computer marketplace by neophytes

Amazon.com/author/brianwkelly

Brian W. Kelly has written 262 books including this one.

Thank you for buying this one.

Others can be found at amazon.com/author/brianwkelly